Let the House of God Be Built

Let the House of God Be Built

The Story and Testimony of Halford House

Lance Lambert

LANCE LAMBERT MINISTRIES

Richmond, Virginia, USA

Previously published by:
New Wine Press
Copyright © 2012

ISBN: 978-1-68389-095-9
www.lancelambert.org

Contents

Foreword

The story of how we discovered Halford House is in itself remarkable. The purchase and the finance required for its restoration and renovation and the miraculous way the Lord provided it, only makes the story more extraordinary. If we add to all of this the provision of its furniture and its furnishings, and the miraculous escape of the workmen from injury and death, we have a testimony to the absolute faithfulness of the Lord.

It was only natural that we who were involved in the story should begin to ask the Lord: What was the meaning behind it? Why did He do all this? It is this enquiry, and the answer the Lord gave, which has led to the writing of this book.

It became clear to us that the story of this house was not an ordinary one. The Lord revealed to us that He was using it as a sign of a deep burden on His heart. That burden of God was the building of His House, His Dwelling Place, or Resting Place. The finding of Halford House—its recovery, rebuilding and renovation—was an illustration of what He desires for those whom He has redeemed. It was that desire which lay behind the creation of the universe, of our planet, and of mankind. When man fell, it was this same intense desire of the Lord which led to Calvary and to our redemption. Through the salvation which the Lord Jesus won for us, God's aim is to make us His Eternal Home.

The story of Halford House began sixty years ago. Most of those who were part of the original story are now with the Lord. Recently, the Lord spoke to me about setting down in writing my recollections of the story before I myself go to be with Him. I have taken the title of this book from the decree of Cyrus concerning the recovery and rebuilding of the Temple, the House of the Lord in Jerusalem. It is recorded in Ezra 5:15 KJV: *Let the house of God be built.*

My prayer and desire is that the Lord will use the testimony of Halford House, its rebuilding and restoration, to bring illumination and understanding of God's Purpose for the Church. The first six chapters recount the story of its restoration, recovery and the birth of the fellowship. The last six chapters and the epilogue deal with the lessons we learnt.

I wish to thank certain people who have been part of this endeavour: Nathan Gosling of the UK for the work he has done in reducing the whole story to printed form. Katherine Pittman of the USA for transcribing the original testimony I gave of the Halford House story and editing the initial transcript, and Helen Reiss for proof reading the manuscript. I also should thank Richard Briggs of the UK and Mark Norris of the USA for looking after the practical work of the house in Naxos, Greece whilst we were writing.

Lance Lambert
Jerusalem March 2012

1.
Born out of Spiritual Travail

The whole story of Halford House began with a group of people who became deeply burdened for the area in which they were living. At the most there were eight people involved. All of the group were young people in their late teens or early twenties apart from Ernest and Dora Townshend. None of us were famous or exceptional in talent. Ken and Gill Douglas and Eileen Johnson are now safely with the Lord, as well as Ernest and Dora Townshend. My sister Teresa and I are the only ones still remaining of the original eight.

The Holy Spirit's Burden

It was a colossal burden that was conceived in us by the Holy Spirit which would not let us rest. I had some experience of intercession whilst in Egypt and had seen a number of my fellow servicemen come to the Lord. However none of us, including myself, had ever been involved in intense corporate intercession.

I had witnessed it with two elderly sisters who had prayed for situations all over the Middle East, and this had deeply impacted me. I returned from Egypt in August 1951. I had spent three years in the Royal Air Force and experienced genuine fellowship amongst those who were believers in Egypt. When I returned to Britain and to the Richmond Upon Thames area, I felt like a "fish out of water." It was as though God had no home in Richmond. There were plenty of evangelical places of worship, and all the evangelical paraphernalia that went with it, but little spiritual building of the House of the Lord. All eight of us shared the same burden. Although we did not fully understand it, the Holy Spirit placed on all our hearts Isaiah, chapter 62:1–3 and 6–7. This became an intense burden with no relief and no escape, except through intercession.

The Hebrides Revival 1949–1952

At that time all the talk in evangelical circles was about the Hebrides Revival. Between 1949 and 1952 a widespread revival swept through those islands in answer to the prayer of some of God's people. There were two elderly sisters, Peggy and Christine Smith, who received a burden from the Lord from which they could not escape. They were eighty-four and eighty-two years old. Peggy was blind and her sister was almost bent double with arthritis. As a result they could not attend worship and turned their little cottage into a sanctuary of intercession. Night and day they sought the Lord. He gave them the promise:

For I will pour water upon him that is thirsty, and streams upon the dry ground; I will pour my Spirit upon thy seed, and my blessing upon thine offspring (Isaiah 44:3).

They took this Scripture and prayed it into fulfilment, standing with the Lord until He performed it. There was also a group of men in the same district who met together in a barn to intercede for the same awakening and revival. They also received a promise from the Lord that:

If my people, who are called by My name, shall humble themselves, and pray, and seek My face, and turn from their wicked ways; then will I hear from heaven, and will forgive their sin, and will heal their land (II Chronicles 7:14).

In the same manner as the two elderly sisters, they persisted in intercession until it happened. These two sisters and these brothers had understood a vitally strategic essential in intercession. They had understood what the Lord meant when He gave us the pattern prayer in Matthew 6:9—13, and in particular the words: "Thy kingdom come. Thy will be done, as in heaven, so on earth." This kind of intercession which resulted in the Hebrides Revival came as a consequence of their understanding of the will of God. First, they had the Word of God and the revelation of His will for the Hebrides, and secondly, by the power of the Holy Spirit and the grace of God they prayed it into being.

When the Holy Spirit was poured out upon those islands, men and women were saved everywhere. Shepherds in the hills, who were caring for their sheep, fell on their faces and were saved.

Fishermen fell on the decks of their fishing boats and got saved. Likewise, many were saved in meetings and others in their homes and cottages. There were many outstanding miracles which took place during those days.

The story of the Hebrides Revival had an enormous challenge for the eight of us. If the Lord could do it in the Hebrides, could He not do it in the Thames valley? I had read *Charles Finney's Lectures on Revival*, and said to the other seven, "If you want to be disturbed, you should read, in particular, the chapter on *ploughing up the fallow ground*." It had deeply disturbed me because Finney had said that if we want awakening and revival, we have a responsibility to break up the hard ground in our lives. It was exactly what had happened in the lives of those sisters and brothers who prayed into existence the move of the Lord in the Hebrides. For example, amongst the group of men that met in the barn was a young deacon who rose and quoted Psalm 24:3—4: "Who shall ascend into the hill of the Lord? And who shall stand in His holy place? He that hath clean hands, and a pure heart; who hath not lifted up his soul unto vanity, nor sworn deceitfully. He shall receive the blessing from the Lord." (AV).

Turning to the others he said: "Brethren, it seems to me just so much humbug to be waiting and praying as we are if we ourselves are not rightly related to God." Then lifting his hands towards heaven he cried: "Oh God, are my hands clean? Is my heart pure?" He got no further but fell prostrate to the floor, an awareness of God filled the barn, and the power of the Holy Spirit was let loose in their lives.

The eight of us talked together about breaking up the fallow ground. We wondered whether the burden we had was truly from the Lord, or whether it was emotional, a result of all the talk about the Hebrides Revival. We therefore covenanted together to do an extraordinary thing; we would not speak about revival, read about revival, or even pray about revival for one whole month. If at the end of that one month this burden was still with us in the same power we would know it was from the Lord. Thus for the whole month of August 1951, we neither spoke about revival, nor read about it, neither discussed it, nor even prayed about it. At the end of that month we found that the burden in us was greater than ever, it was like a pain in our spirits. I was only a young Christian, but I can only describe it as incurable pain. I could not get it out of my system. It was there like a deep, deep anguish of the Holy Spirit.

Costly and Committed Intercession

On the first day of September 1951, we started to pray, and we prayed every evening of September, October, November and December until Christmas of 1951. Our times of prayer began just after 7.00 pm and went on until between 10.00 and 10.30 pm. In the middle of it we had the severest smog that London had ever known in which 3000 people died. Fog is thick mist and is natural; smog is a mixture of smoke and fumes combined with mist, and can be a killer. For 10 days we could not see across the street. At one point, during those days, all transport ceased, but it never stopped our prayer. We walked about three miles across Richmond to the home of Ernest and Dora Townshend. In those times of prayer and intercession, we were never less than two and never more than eight. We prayed every night and on

Saturday we would pray from 2 o'clock until 6 o'clock, so that we could attend the young people's meeting in the church to which many of us belonged. We also got permission to pray in the vestry of that church on Sunday evenings so that we were not a faction or division, and we prayed for the service as well. In fact, we never cancelled a single session of prayer during those four months.

One Single Burden for Prayer

We only had one single burden in our intercession and we never deviated from that burden. We did not pray for Nepal, or China, or Australia, or even Japan; we simply prayed for Richmond and the Thames valley. Every evening of prayer lasted no less than three hours. Now we all know how hard it is to sustain prayer for half an hour even when there are many items that need to be prayed through. As I recall that time, I am still amazed at it. It is like a dream. However, I remember that when we began to pray we could do nothing else but pray. At the end of those three hours it was rather like a tank that had been drained of all its water, and one could get up from one's knees with a feeling of relief. Notwithstanding, the next morning the tank was full again. One felt uncomfortable, as if one had a pain inside and the only way to let it out was in intercession. I have often likened it to physical birth. Once an embryo has been conceived it grows and there is no full relief until birth.

It was my first real experience of corporate intercession on this level. It was the Spirit of God who was in us keeping alive a burden. Our intercession covered the whole varied life of the Richmond area. We prayed for all kinds of different places and those who were in them—for example: public houses, every kind of shady joint, bars, nightclubs, hospitals, schools, and colleges, for local government, for the mayors of both Richmond and Twickenham, and of course, for churches, both alive and dead. We had a burden and it was a two-fold burden; firstly, that God would do a new thing in His people, and secondly, that He would start to save the unsaved straight off the street. We had no idea that one of the nightclubs we prayed for, the Astor Club, would be closed down by the police for immorality, and we would actually get possession of it and meet there for one whole year. That possibility never entered our heads when we were praying for it!

Koinonia

Those four months of prayer with the same burden were an incredible experience. We felt as if we were in a sovereign flow of God's power. As we have already pointed out, we all know how hard it is to pray for one subject for even half an hour. We prayed, however, for virtually one subject from all angles for three hours every single day right up to Christmas 1951. Out of that came Koinonia, the interdenominational "get together" of young people in the Richmond area just to worship the Lord, to wait upon the Lord and fellowship together. We would take a subject and discuss it together and then have a Bible study on it. The commencement of these sessions was on the first Friday of January 1952. We called it Koinonia, which is the New Testament Greek word for "fellowship" or "sharing" or "having something in common." Within a month of the first session, nearly every evangelical church in the area was represented in spite of it not being advertised. Our naming of this gathering of young people elicited quite an amount of criticism from older Christians in the churches. They said it was a Russian word, and they thought that because I was in my early twenties I was politically leaning towards Marxism, and that this would be a great danger for the young people in the fellowship.

The Bible studies in Koinonia, by the grace of God and the anointing of the Holy Spirit, became life-transforming for the young people who attended. The first Bible study in 1952 was entitled: "The supremacy and pre-eminence of the Lord Jesus." This one study seemed to impact permanently everyone who came. We spoke of the Lord Jesus as the centre and circumference of the Bible, the centre and circumference of the natural creation, the centre and circumference of salvation, the centre and circumference of the Christian life, and the centre and circumference of the Church. This one study probably had more impact than any other that followed. Other subjects, for example, were the Lord's Table, Communion, Believers' Baptism, the unity of all believers, etc. Many young people got saved during the Bible studies. There was such power in the fellowship. The whole session was alive to God, and we expected Him to speak to us.

After prayer and fellowship together, we decided that we would have three Fridays a month for Bible study and one Friday a month for a kind of evangelistic outreach. We called this time a "squash," because so many people would crowd in. In fact, the first one we had at the Townshend's home was so crowded that we had young people all over the ground floor in all the rooms, up the stairs and into the bedrooms. We had made a stipulation that only those who brought an unsaved friend could come to the squash; the others were to go to the prayer meeting. A pastor of one of the fellowships spoke on that occasion. Three people got saved that night. We also felt that we should take places that the world widely used and with which it was comfortable. So we took the restaurant of the Ritz cinema, we took the Cadena restaurant which was well known and in both of these we had an evangelistic meeting.

The most unusual place was when we took the largest Thames launch steamer and sailed up the river Thames from Richmond to Hampton Court and back. Once everybody was on board they could not leave and a number got saved that night on the steamer! Each of these evangelistic times was preceded by a number of sessions of prayer. One young man, Ron Howes, who was a Congregationalist but unsaved, came along to the sessions of prayer and found the Lord. He married Mildred Perkins and they were faithful in the contribution they made to the fellowship from almost the beginning—Mildred in playing the piano at the meetings in the early years and Ron looking after the practical side of the house and the stewarding.

The Lifting of the Prayer Burden

The most extraordinary fact was that with the advent of Koinonia the prayer burden that had been so intense in the eight of us lifted. At first we wondered whether we were retreating from the original call which God had given us. However, when we tried to pray, it was just words. The impetus of the burden had lifted. We fellowshipped together and realised that to carry on with the prayer burden would be like "flogging a dead horse." Later with the wisdom of hindsight we understood from the Lord that Koinonia, and what followed, was the answer to our intercession. From this we learnt one single but vital lesson. As in everything to do with our salvation—our Christian life and our church life—so it is with the ministry of intercession; it begins with Christ, it is empowered by Christ, and it ends with Christ.

A Church Within a Church

The criticism and condemnation that we received from the majority of Christians in our area was enormous. The rumours became facts in the eyes of many. We were accused of being Mormons, Russellites (Jehovah Witnesses), and even of having tendencies towards Marxism. It was claimed that we worshipped the devil, that the money came from the devil, and the people converted amongst us were converted to the devil! Is it any wonder that these young people, numbering now approximately 100, were horrified, especially those who had been recently saved amongst us! They knew the truth and could not believe how real Christians could say such things.

I was also accused of giving illicit sex instruction to the young people during those times! The accusations became so bad that a titled lady friend of mine, a missionary to India who was on board a boat going out to that country, was asked by a bishop of the Church of England: "Is it really true that Lance led a group of young men and smashed the manse of the pastor?"

I remember once at one of the Koinonia sessions in Berwyn road, a young lady shot in. She never took off her hat or her coat, but she went straight into a corner and sat bolt upright in a chair, took a notebook out and a pencil at the ready. Gradually, as the time went on she relaxed more and more. She had been sent in by a Sunday school superintendent of one of the churches of the area to take notes of the séance we were supposedly having. No wonder she was nervous. However, she got so blessed that she stayed. The superintendent then said: "Lance has a devilishly hypnotic influence over people".

The pastor of one of the largest and most powerful evangelical churches in the area to which I belonged asked to see me and the other leaders of Koinonia. He gave us an ultimatum; either we went into the organisation of the Baptist church or all who were members of his church would be expelled. That came as a thunderbolt to us. We were confused and not sure what course to take. We had at that time adopted the normal Baptist and Congregational practice of a majority vote. I gave them a pep talk on not splitting the church, which was a famous church and had missionaries all over the world. A narrow majority felt we should go back into the organisation, but a minority felt it was wrong to go back. Now it turned out that the ones who said it would be wrong were right! The moment we went back into the church organisation and had our meetings announced from the pulpit, it was as if all the power left us. A curtain seemed to have come down upon us all.

We realised that we had made a huge mistake, and through it we learnt one of the greatest lessons it is possible to learn. We do not put matters right by retracing our steps and seeking to undo the mistake we have made! Why did we make the mistake in the first place? It was for the very reason that we did not seek the Lord. When the Lord said to the children of Israel "go over into the land," and they would not, the Lord said, "I am no longer with you, because you have disobeyed me." Then they said, "We will go over." Moses said, "Do not go over because you made your first mistake when you did not listen to the Lord and trust Him. Now you think you can rectify that mistake by simply undoing it instead of hearing the Lord and in faith obeying Him."

From what we learnt in that situation we threw out the majority vote and went by the principle of unanimity. We sought the Lord in prayer and heard Him; we were to wait for His direction. Within a month the same pastor came and said, "It seems to me that this coming into the church organisation has divided it more than your being outside of it. Therefore, I think it is better if you take the whole thing outside." Our rejoicing knew no measure. Once again the power of God came to us, and our gatherings were full of life.

Nevertheless we were a church within a church. Less and less fellow believers would speak to us. They would not shake our hands or greet us in any way. My old Sunday school teacher would turn his head the other way. People I had known from the day I was saved turned their back on me. They would not say good morning or good evening to me. I was not alone in this treatment. We all had this kind of experience. Many of these believers were those we loved very greatly and we had received much from them spiritually. It was for all of us a time of anguish. We had become a church within a church! We decided that we should seek the Lord. So for three weeks we sought His face—some of us with fasting. We said we will not make a majority block decision; we will each one do what the Lord says. There were 18 of us out of approximately 100 who felt they should resign from the churches of which they were members. The rest felt they should remain.

Reduced to Eighteen Believers

It was not easy to be reduced from 100 to 18, and at the beginning we felt lost and confused. Everyone, it seemed to us, spoke against us. However, we took the one step that we had discovered to be the answer in any situation, however difficult it could be. Together we sought the Lord. We were, apart from the Townshends, all young people in our teens and twenties. Dora Townshend's sisters, Helen and Grace Wheelwright, joined us at that time. Suddenly we were alone without the structure and organisation to which we had been accustomed. We were "green" youngsters and had no idea what to do. We just fell into the arms of God because for us there was no other possibility. It was the best position to be in! All the illumination and the revelation that came through His Word and the experiences of Him into which we came began from this position. The Lord took us as little children and led us all the way. Literally, He led us by the hand.

As we sought the Lord He gave us His Word, confirmed by more than one witness. In other words, the Scriptures which He gave us, as we were seeking Him, were on the heart of more than one person amongst us.

The first was: "Depart ye, depart ye, go ye out from thence, touch no unclean thing; go ye out of the midst of her; cleanse yourselves, ye that bear the vessels of the Lord. For ye shall not go out in haste, neither shall ye go by flight: for the

Lord will go before you; and the God of Israel will be your rearward." (Isaiah 52:11—12).

A second was: "Therefore thus saith the Lord. If thou return, then will I bring thee again, that thou mayest stand before me; and if thou take forth the precious from the vile, thou shalt be as my mouth: they shall return unto thee, but thou shalt not return unto them. And I will make thee unto this people a fortified brazen wall; and they shall fight against thee, but they shall not prevail against thee; for I am with thee to save thee and to deliver thee, saith the Lord." (Jeremiah 15:19—20).

The third was: "The word of the Lord also came unto me, saying, Son of man, thou dwellest in the midst of the rebellious house, that have eyes to see, and see not, that have ears to hear, and hear not; for they are a rebellious house. Therefore, thou son of man, prepare thee stuff for removing, and remove by day in their sight; and thou shalt remove from thy place to another in their sight: it may be they will consider, though they are a rebellious house." (Ezekiel 12:1—3).

These Scriptures were a great encouragement to us. They confirmed the position we had taken. At that time we did not know our Bibles so well, and it was a great comfort to us that through some obscure parts of His Word He spoke to us. We understood clearly from the Lord that we were never to go back, but that we were to go forward with Him. Secondly, we understood that we were to remain within sight of the churches we had left.

At the beginning we met in a home. The first time we ever met for the Lord's Table was on a very foggy morning in November 1952 at 20 Berwyn Road, East Sheen. We were about 20 people on that first occasion around the Lord's Table. I spoke from what the Lord had given me in Proverbs 3:5—6: "Trust in the Lord with all thy heart, and lean not upon thine own understanding: In all thy ways acknowledge Him, and He will direct thy paths." As we simply trusted the Lord and His directions and did not lean upon our own understanding, the Lord led us into everything.

One of the rumours that went round the churches was that I had always wanted a church. It was, so it was claimed, my idea from the beginning, and it was an obsession of mine! However, I can honestly say that it had never occurred to me or to any of us to have a church. We never thought we would move out from the others. We thought the new thing that God was going to do would be *in* all these churches. It would be new life, new power; it would be revival and awakening. It was a terrible shock to us when we found ourselves finally outside of it all.

We were on our own and totally ostracised. No one would touch us. Yet in the Lord's wisdom it protected us from being swamped by multitudes of spectators, the "Sunday go to meeting Christians." Those who came to us were either saved in our midst or had run the gauntlet. They were Christians who were hungry for something more of the Lord. Brother T. Austin-Sparks was one who ran the gauntlet, because he had much the same experience as we did. We enjoyed his fellowship and that of other brothers from the Christians meeting at Honor Oak.

2.
A House on Richmond Hill

The Community Centre

After a few months of meeting in the Townshends home, we felt that we really had to meet somewhere else. We were wearing out the home of those dear believers. Therefore, we began seriously to seek the Lord as to where this place should be. In one of the Scriptures which the Lord had given us, He had said: ..."thou shalt remove from thy place to another in their sight." (see Ezekiel 12:1–3). It was at this point that we heard of the Community Centre which was next door to the synagogue in the heart of the town of Richmond. It was certainly within sight of the church to which I had belonged. I went to inquire of it and they said they had a room on the top floor that they could rent us for a reasonable price. It was the Royal Richmond and Twickenham Photographic Society's room. The walls were covered with the most beautiful photographs, some of which we had to turn toward the wall before we could decently meet in that room. In fact, it was one of our steward's jobs to go through the pictures before anyone arrived and turn certain ones toward the wall and later turn them back when all of us had left! However, to reach this room one had to first go down into the basement, pass through all the stage props, go through a very ill-lit cellar, and then up some rickety steps to the top floor. Sometimes the person who was supposed to open up on a Sunday did not arrive until about five minutes past eleven, or even later, and we were supposed to be meeting at 11am. These drawbacks disturbed us, but we accepted it because of what the Lord had said.

Elders and Deacons

During our time at the Community Centre the Lord blessed the fellowship. We grew in numbers and several got saved. We met there every Sunday morning and evening and had prayer meetings and Bible studies in private homes. It was there also that we made a big mistake. We appointed elders and deacons because we saw it as a Biblical pattern. The pattern was not wrong; it was the way we appointed them which was incorrect. We discovered later that the apostle Paul never appointed elders or deacons on his first trip, but on his second, which was often 18 months to two years later. In other words, he waited to see how the believers were developing, and he watched for the growth of spiritual character. The body of Christ is spiritually organic. A believer who is to be an elder or a deacon grows in such a way that it will be clear to all the members of the body that the believer concerned has the right character and spiritual gift. We learnt one of the greatest lessons about the Church through this mistake. We learnt that the

Church is in the resurrection life of Christ and the Holy Spirit is the one who makes the will of the Head known to the members.

The Taking of the Astor Club

Although we had been blessed greatly by our time in the Community Centre, we realised that there were many drawbacks, and thus we began to look for another venue. On one occasion I was looking at different places in the centre of Richmond when I saw a little notice: "Apply to Burton's for the place above." Just before that I had met old Mrs. Caiger, John and Arthur Caiger's mother. She was a most godly woman and a strong prayer intercessor. She said, "What are you doing?"

I said, "I am looking for a place for us to hold our meetings."

"My dear" she said, "That is a big work."

I said, "Well I am just about to give up."

"Do not give up!" she said, "I am shopping, but I will pray."

I said, "Whilst you are shopping?"

"Oh, no problem at all! I will pray whilst I am shopping. Do not give up!"

The place that was advertised on that little note was a nightclub, the Astor Club, for which we had prayed in those four months in 1951. It had been closed down by the police for immorality. This place was in the old arcade that had been bombed during the Blitz of London in the Second World War, and was left more or less in ruins. Anyway I went to Burton's, the tailors and a big man came out and asked me: "What do you want?"

I said, "I have come about the advertisement."

He said, "What are you?"

I said, "We are a group of Christian young people."

"What do you want it for?"

"For meetings," I said.

"That is a very strange thing," he said.

"I understood it was not on the market," I said.

He said, "An hour ago I received the go ahead to rent it! I will give you the first option for one pound a week for the whole lot. But you must be prepared to be tipped out at a week's notice."

Now the Richmond council had an argument with Burton's, the tailors, so although they owned the property the council was blocking their development of it. We understood from one of our brothers who was working for the council that there was no chance of Burton's being given the go ahead for probably fourteen years at least. So we took it. It was on the High Street of Richmond, opposite the post office. (Eventually it was developed when Marks and Spencer's purchased it from Burton's, and they were in great favour with the council).

When we took it we had to clean up the whole place. We had to shut our eyes while scrubbing the graffiti off the walls. It was not a very nice place. We had a service in which we spiritually sanctified the whole area, and in particular the premises which the Astor club had occupied. Of course, some of the local Christians became very upset about us. "Oh," they said, "first they go to cinemas, then they take steamers, now they are meeting in a nightclub. What next! Where else will that boy lead them?" We had a new carpet for the main room, and huge interlined curtains for the very large windows to shut out the noise of traffic. The material for those curtains came from an Auschwitz survivor in the town, and the lady who made the curtains was another survivor who gave the making of the curtains as a gift. This place was absolutely central, we were able to go out and "fish" people in from High Street and other nearby streets, and a number got saved. We were now able to have both the prayer meeting and the Bible study in this new place.

Was the Lord Moving Us?

We were only there for a year when suddenly one day in the winter the water poured in through the roof. Now what was the point of us mending the roof, indeed doing any of the necessary repairs, when we could be tipped out with a week's notice? Unofficially, we could be there for fourteen years, but we wondered. Then suddenly I came in one day and found a very officious man walking about. Later he became a good friend, but at the time he was extremely overbearing. He was going around tapping walls and ceilings. I thought he was nuts. "Excuse me," I said, "what are you doing?"

"Excuse me," he said, "have you got permission to meet in this place?"

I said, "What has that got to do with you?"

He replied, "I happen to be the chief building inspector for this area. And I understand you are meeting here as a church; have you got permission? For one thing that whole fire escape has got to be fire proofed; we can close you down you know!"

I said, "I did not know anything about this."

He said, "Then we had better get moving." After that he became reasonably pleasant and said we had to do this and that and the other.

When we got a man to look at the roof, he said it would cost at least £200. When we asked about fireproofing the staircase from asbestos, he said that would be about £250; in all £450. As always we prayed about it. We could spend £450 on the place and be tipped out within a week. Was the Lord moving us on?

The Pillar of Cloud and Fire on the Move

It was then that someone in the prayer meeting said, "The Pillar of Cloud and Fire is moving; we must follow." And someone else took it up in prayer, and still another. I was really upset. I thought, "We have only just got here; we have just bought a fitted carpet and put up the interlined curtains; surely the Lord is not moving us on. Would the carpet fit another place, and the huge curtains?" Then someone else suddenly read a Scripture. It turned out that she had never read this Scripture before, but she gave it:

> And it shall come to pass in the latter days, that the mountain of the Lord's house shall be established on the top of the mountains, and shall be exalted above the hills; and all nations shall flow unto it. And many peoples shall go and say, Come ye, and let us go up to the mountain of the Lord, to the house of the God of Jacob; and he shall teach us of His ways, and we will walk in His paths: for out of Zion shall go forth the law, and the word of the Lord from Jerusalem (Isaiah 2:2—3).

To my amazement one other person had the same passage and read it, and then to add to my horror someone else read from Micah 4:1—2, which is the exact same Scripture as the Isaiah verses. I thought that our prayer meeting was crazy. There was no mountain in Richmond, only Richmond Hill. How could these two Scriptures have anything to do with our local situation about finding a house in which to meet? Was it even possible to apply these Scriptures to our local situation? After all, it was originally given concerning the Temple of God in Jerusalem. Nevertheless, everyone in the prayer meeting seemed to feel that the Lord was speaking to us about a house somewhere on Richmond Hill.

Lord Hore-Belisha's Home

We took the whole matter to the Lord and sought Him until we became unanimous. The Lord was indicating a house on Richmond Hill! Thus we began a search for this "House on the hill." We discovered from estate agents a number of houses and went to investigate. One of those houses had belonged to Lord Hore-Belisha. It was a magnificent house with a great garden, a ballroom with white panelling, gilt decoration and parquet flooring. It seemed the perfect place to meet. There was another large room lined—ceiling, walls, and floor with cobalt blue Italian mosaic and a sunken roman bath which seemed to be a perfect baptistery. It appeared to clinch the matter for us. In 1953–54, this was going for £7500. We prayed about it, but not a penny came in.

Ancaster House

We also looked at Ancaster House, a beautiful large house on the top of Richmond Hill, with its own garden and a gate into

Richmond Park. It had the most beautiful Cumberland green slate roof. Once again we prayed about it. It was valued at between £7000 and £8000, but nothing came. We looked at other houses also, but it seemed remarkable to us that not a single pound was given towards any of them.

Halford House

On a certain Tuesday morning I woke up with a sense that I had to do something about a house in which we could meet. I had spoken about a certain house on Richmond Green which could hardly be called on Richmond Hill. It was for sale, but we had not looked at it. Then I did something which was not natural to me. I decided to go through all the estate agents in East Twickenham and Richmond, one by one. Everywhere I went I got the same reply that there was nothing available.

Finally I came to Chancellors which was near Richmond Railway station. As I went in a young man stood up and said, "Yes sir, can I do anything for you?" I explained what we needed and said I had noticed in their window the house on Richmond Green advertised, the house which I had wondered about. He told me that they had finally sold the house only that morning and greatly below the asking price. I had explained to him that we were young people and were looking for a house to purchase in which to meet. He said that at present there was nothing available. "Nevertheless," he said, "let me take down the details." He asked for my address. As soon as he learnt the address his attitude changed. The family home was in the most highly rated area of East Twickenham.

It was at that point that an old gentleman, who was sitting in the rear of the office, stood up and said how sorry he was that we had not come in earlier. I was only in my early twenties, and I reckoned the older gentleman with his white flowing hair was at least eighty, as I am now! "We do not have anything suitable for you at present," he said, "but I have no doubt that we shall find something." I got up to go and had my back to the old gentleman when he said, "Just wait, sir, something comes to my mind!" But then it was as if he was talking to himself. As I wheeled round to face him, he was holding his hand to his head, and saying, "Oh, he would not be interested in that place, especially if he was prepared to pay the price of the house on the Green!"

I broke into his conversation with himself, saying, "Where is this house?"

"Oh sir," he said, "be advised, I do not know why I thought of it. It has been on our Dead Book for thirteen years. No sir, it is not for you. It has wood boring beetles, dry rot and no damp course. It is virtually derelict. Sir, it would be a wild goose chase if you went up there. Wait for us and we will find you the right place."

Then I said, "I am not so sure about that! I am rather interested. Where is this house?"

"It is on Halford Road," he said.

I told him that I had known Halford Road since I was a child (it was where Aunty Ella lived).

He said that it was a School of Art and Science.

I said, "I cannot recall any such place on Halford Road."

He said, "Sir, it has been there since 1710!"

"Well," I said, "I am very interested."

"Oh sir," he replied, "do be advised. You are just wasting your time. It will only be a load of trouble."

"No," I exclaimed. "I would like to see it."

"Alright," he replied. "If that is what you want, all right! I will send someone up with the key." Then we arranged for the time to be at 2 pm that same day.

The Condition of Halford House

Thus at 2 pm Ken Douglas, Ernest Townshend and myself waited outside the door. It was not one of the young men that came and certainly not the old man, but a young lad with a huge key. He inserted the key in the front door and had to more or less swing on it to open it. The door creaked open and the first thing that hit us was the smell. There were holes in the floor; we had to be careful where we walked. Fungus was growing on the walls. Plaster had fallen away onto the ground. There was no electricity, only gas brackets. When we went upstairs to what is now the library, the handle of the door came away in our hands. Then when we got hold of the door, a whole part of the door came away and crumbled into powder. I went through the whole place thinking, "Oh no, Lord." A Scripture came to me: "Every good gift and every perfect gift is from above, coming down from the Father of lights." (James 1:17a). I thought, this is not good or perfect, and therefore can it be a gift from God?! All I could think about was the amount of work we would have to do. The other brothers, however, were amazed. Here is this place in the centre of Richmond, with much space. It would be possible to seat 100 people in the ground floor room and if the upstairs was renovated, at least 300.

The Purchase of Halford House

It is noteworthy that as a fellowship nearly every major move we had to make in our history always originated on the day we had our main prayer meeting. It was a Tuesday and that evening was our main prayer time. So we three brothers decided to present to the whole fellowship what had happened during the day. We would not tell them how we felt in order not to influence them, but to let the Lord lead all of us clearly as a body. The trustees of Halford House wanted £3000 for it. We all sought the Lord and became of one mind that this was the place. It was on Richmond Hill, but on the lower part of it. We came to a unanimous decision to offer £200. One must remember that except for one family, we were all in our teens and twenties, and most of us students. To us therefore, £200 was an enormous sum of money. It was thus in faith that we sent the letter offering £200. We received a reply almost immediately. Could we reconsider because they felt our offer was too little? We did more than reconsider; we sought the Lord, decided to double the sum, and added the £50 we had in hand which came to £450. We received the trustee's response within a week. They said they believed we were going to do a good work amongst young people, and that although the sum was small they would accept the offer providing we paid in cash within seven days.

Now we were overjoyed, but we realised we had only seven days in which to pay. We had taken a position financially that was absolute. We never asked for money, we never advertised our needs, and those of us who worked for the fellowship never asked for wages, but trusted the Lord. Within the week the £400 came, including a gift from New York of £23 from a sister who had heard about a work in Richmond, but did not know about our need.

What is amazing is the fact that if we had paid £450 for renewing the old nightclub premises, which we were in, we would have lost everything. Literally, two months later, when we were just about to come into Halford House, every person in the whole of the old arcade, all the shopkeepers there, were suddenly given one week's notice to get out. Overnight Burton's sold the property to Mark's and Spencer's who were in favour with the council and they gave them the go ahead for re-development. We would have spent £450 on a new roof and fireproofing, and the whole thing would have been pulled down. Some of the shopkeepers were angry with us. I remember one of them whom I had known from childhood, saying, "Fancy you Christians treating your friends like that!" He was Jewish. "You Christians can never be trusted," he said, "you knew." I said, "we did not know!"

He said, "Come off it! Of course you knew! You have been searching for a house these last months. They gave you the tip off because you are a Christian organisation."

I said, "No, they did not. We prayed about it and God gave us the tip off." Later he gave me a beautiful oil painting of the Austrian Alps, which I treasure. He was the only one who had managed to negotiate a sixteen year lease, the rest of us were given a one week notice. To move out he got a handsome sum of money for each of those years.

Thus we would have spent £450 and been tipped out and the whole lot pulled down for re-development. Instead, the Lord provided £450 for the purchase of Halford House. The Pillar of Cloud and Fire had certainly moved, and by the grace of God we moved with Him. We hardly knew what we had purchased. In the residential part of the house lived an old music professor and his wife. They had an old dog that was white with age and used to howl every time we sang a hymn. They also had a cat, so old that it had a relaxed back and its stomach dragged on the ground, and an old hen that was the last of fourteen hens they had owned during the war years. These three slept together in the same basket. The Hullah's paid £1.50 per week for renting the residential part of the house and the garden. We had also inherited what we thought was an artist, an aged lady in her late eighties, who lived across the garden in a one room building with her cats. All of this we were to discover little by little.

The Remarkable Story of Margaret Trickey

It was one thing to have bought Halford House in a miracle worked by God; it was another matter to consider how the house would be cared for and managed. Margaret Trickey was a gift of God to the fellowship at Halford House. When we bought the property we wondered how we were going to care for it. Margaret offered herself, saying that she believed the Lord had spoken to her clearly. She had joined the fellowship whilst we were meeting in the Astor Club.

When Margaret was in her early twenties, she contracted Poliomyelitis. Her condition was so bad that she could not move a single part of her body except her eyeballs. At one point the doctors thought that she would be in an Iron Lung. Amazingly, the Lord healed her! However the doctors who cared for her said that she would only be able to work in certain spheres, such as a children's nurse. She would never be able to shoulder a strenuous job.

Margaret was born in Kaifeng, Honan, China to missionary parents. Her mother died two weeks after giving birth to her. She was one of seven children. She came to the Lord early and devoted her life to Him. She was greatly influenced by Brother T. Austin-Sparks.

It was only natural that we brothers wondered whether Margaret would be able to cope with the heavy duties of caring for and managing Halford House. As we sought the Lord about this, we became convinced that it was a genuine call of God she had heard. We prayed for an especial anointing of grace and power for her.

The years that followed proved that Margaret was called of God. Not only did she look after the house but she cooked for all who were there daily. We had students from many nations living with us and seeking to learn from the Lord at Halford House. There could be anywhere between 10 and 20 people for lunch each day. Margaret cooked beautiful meals on a very small budget. Everyone used to wonder how she could do it. Except for periodic migraines, which would lay her out for a day, she shouldered all the onerous duties.

Spiritually, she knew the Lord in a deep and powerful way and was a very real and alive contribution to the life of the fellowship. Her miraculous story is interwoven with the history of the fellowship of believers at Halford House. She was an eye witness of most of the miracles which God worked for us.

3.
The Recovery and Restoration of Halford House

The state of the building was deplorable. There were two parts to the building—the residential house in which Professor Hullah Brown and his wife lived, and the other side which had been a School of Art and Science. Although there was much dry rot and wood boring beetle on the residential side, it was much worse on the School of Art side. On that side there was also no electricity nor fresh water. We were therefore faced with a mammoth task.

The First Essential Renovation

The primary and essential reconstruction work on the meeting side of the house was done by a firm of builders. There were four basic and main matters with which we had to cope. Firstly, we had to have the foundation renewed and reinforced. We had understood that there was no damp course, but the builders discovered that there was an old ancient eighteenth century one. This was the cause of some of the dry rot. Secondly was the roof which, of course, leaked badly. The place had been empty for thirty years and derelict for thirteen. The water which had leaked from the roof had caused much of the dry rot and had to be dealt with immediately. It meant a new roof and the replacing of some timbers. The third matter was electricity; there was no electricity in the building. Everything had been with gas lighting, long since defunct. The fourth matter was the water piping and the bringing of good fresh water into the building. These were the four basic and essential items of reconstruction.

The Cost of This Essential Recovery and Its Supply

For this work the builders presented us with a quote of £1250. It was nearly three times the amount we had paid for the house. We had six weeks in which to find the money. For the whole fellowship it was thrilling to see that without any advertisement, appeals, subtle hints, telephone calls, or letters, every penny of the £1250 came in. We were able to pay all the bills on time. It was a marvellous testimony to the faithfulness of the Lord. It was also a test of faith for the whole fellowship. First, there had been the purchase of the property; and now, secondly, this even greater sum for its basic renovation. The Lord had imprinted on our mind the first time we broke bread together to: "Trust in the Lord with all thy heart, and lean not upon thine own understanding: In all thy ways acknowledge him, and he will direct thy paths." (Proverbs 3:5—6). We had proved His absolute faithfulness.

The Carpet and the Interlined Curtains Were Exact

In the course of this basic restoration we were able to meet in the large downstairs room. The kitchen was in order, as also were the toilets for both men and women, and so was the study. The Lord gave us a wonderful confirmation that the Pillar of Cloud and Fire **had** moved, and that when in faith we followed, we had discovered His full provision. The new fitted carpet from the old premises fitted exactly in the downstairs room without the need of any alteration. The huge interlined curtains fitted exactly the two main windows of that room, also, without having to have any alterations made to them. It all spoke to us of the need to hear the Lord and to follow Him in obedience. For what the Lord commands, He always provides!

The Grandfather Clock of 1710

When we first moved into Halford House we had no chairs to sit on, no tables, nor any kind of furniture. Apart from the metal meeting room chairs, which we had already brought from the previous place of meeting, we had nothing. The first piece of furniture that came to us was an old grandfather clock. This came through a dear old Jewish antique dealer in Richmond, Isaac Wolfe, whom I had known for years. He was a survivor from Auschwitz. There, he had lost his whole original family, his wife and his six children, his grandparents on both sides of the family, his brothers and sisters and their families. All had been gassed a few weeks before the liberation of Auschwitz by the

Red Army. He used to have periodic rows with his second wife. On this occasion he had a terrific row with her about the clock which was lumbering up the hallway of their home. It was in pieces, it did not run, and apparently he was doing nothing about it. She told him that either it had to go, or she would go!

A Grandfather Clock for £3

So "Wolfie" as we affectionately called him, got hold of me in Brewers lane and dragged me into his shop and said: "Do you vant a clock?"

And I said: "No we do not need a clock."

He then said: "But zis is a most vunderful clock! Doesn't the Shul need a clock?"

So I said: "I know it may be a wonderful clock, but we do not need a clock. We need chairs to sit on and tables to eat from."

He said, "You must av zis clock! I only ask £3."

I said, "What is it like?"

"Oh," he said, "it is magnificent."

Now my friend Betty Redman who had the antique shop next door, and whom I had known from childhood, was standing behind him and signalling for me to take it! So I said to Wolfie, "All right, if it helps you, I will take it for £3."

Uncle Jim and the Grandfather Clock

Thus, this grandfather clock came to Halford House. Everyone there sat on the ground and wept with laughter. They said, "You must be nuts! We have nothing to sit on except the metal chairs and no tables to eat on, but you have a grandfather clock; does it go?"

I said, "Wolfie says it will go!"

They said, "How do you know if it will go? He has sold you a dud!"

"Well," I said, "someone will come in and put it right!" Unbelievably, my mother walked in at lunchtime with a friend from Ulster, whom I had known from early childhood as Uncle Jim. They walked around the old house and Uncle Jim said, "What is that down there? It looks like a lovely old clock."

"Yes," I said, "it is a grandfather clock."

"Does it go?" he asked.

"I have no idea," I said.

Uncle Jim then said, "I will take it away and get it going."

"Oh," I said, "I did not know you did anything like that!"

He said, "Clocks are my hobby." And he took it away, repaired it, and it has run beautifully ever since.

Lord Aasquith's French Polisher

Then the most extraordinary thing of all happened. We were cleaning up the downstairs rooms when there was a knocking at the front door. So I went to the front door and there was a strange man looking as if he had stepped out of a story of Dickens. He said, "I am Lord Asquith's French polisher." I said, "Really!" He said, "I believe there is some furniture here to be polished." I said, "Furniture! We have not got any furniture in this place except a few metal chairs." Then I remembered the clock. "We do have the case of an old clock; it is in the kitchen. Come in and have a look." He looked at the clock case. It was black as if it had been painted with some cheap black paint. "I'll get that done for you," he said. Without any more fuss he opened a little bag and started the work. I was in the study and I remember the old gentleman coming across and saying, "Sir, you must come immediately. This is a very valuable clock."

I said, "Is it?"

He said, "Yes. From where did you obtain it?"

I told him I had bought it from an old friend of mine in the town for £3.

"Well," he said, "I am sure it is a catalogued clock." When I looked at it I could not believe what he had done. He had taken all the black rubbish off the clock case, and it revealed a beautiful case. It was a Sheridan piece and a catalogued clock from 1710, the same age as the house. Halford House is a Queen Anne manor house from 1710. Actually, the experts of ancient monuments, who came to look at the house, said that the front porch was dated from 1680. They thought there had been a fire which had destroyed the rest of the house and it had been rebuilt. Halford House is a Grade II ancient monument. It is of great interest because there are few Queen Anne manor houses left. To us young people the grandfather clock was a sign from the Lord that He was with us.

I have said that this clock went beautifully. The only time it stopped was when Brother Bahkt Singh, the great Indian evangelist and Bible teacher, came to speak to us. Now, wherever Bahkt Singh stayed or preached, there was a legend that the clocks stopped! He was certainly not a short preacher! It was indeed true of us, for every time he came the old grandfather clock stopped.

Wolfie could not get over the fact that this clock dated from that time! The whole Jewish community in Richmond used to stop me and say, "Wasn't it funny about Wolfie and the clock?!" The gift of the grandfather clock was the beginning of so much more that the Lord gave in furnishings and in furniture. It was the harbinger of everything else that was to follow.

Brain and Ivy Hare's Wedding

There is not a piece of furniture in the library that was not a miracle. We wanted to get it ready for Brian and Ivy's wedding. They had both come to the Lord amongst us, and they wanted to have the wedding amongst Christians so that there would not be a booze-up. For this reason we needed to complete the renovation of the library which was upstairs. The marriage would take place downstairs in the main room and we planned for the reception to be held in the library. We did not, however, have much time in which to complete it. So we began by sanding the old floor and bees waxing it; however the floor was very sticky. Therefore we had to get carpets for it. We prayed much about the carpets.

Then Jill Douglas's mother, Jessie Manclark, phoned up and said, "Lance, have you thought about going to Hamptons?" And I said, "Hamptons of Kensington are the most expensive carpet people in London!" She said, "Nevertheless, you can get some real bargains there; they are actually having some sales on today. You could get a real bargain. Why don't you phone the manager and ask him?"

Well, I had tried everything else and there was nothing materialising. So I thought I might as well try. We felt we had to have carpets because it seemed wrong to have a wedding reception without them on the floor. So I phoned up and got through to the manager. I said, "Excuse me, we want two medium quality Wilton broad-loom off the same loom, cedar green carpets, 12 x 10 ft."

"Oh," he said, "you have seen our advert."

"No," I said, "I have not seen any advert."

He said, "That is extraordinary; it is in the Evening Standard. Did you not see it? It was out at lunchtime. One of our bargains is 10 x 12 ft. super, quality cedar green carpets. If you come today they will be £120 each, but if you come tomorrow you can have both for £100."

So we went up to Hamptons; Jessie Manclark took me up in her car. As soon as we saw them we knew they were the right carpets. We put down £10 for the deposit because it was all we had. When I came back, there on the desk in the study was the rest—£90 in cash. Another miracle!

The Other Library Furnishings

The old candelabra in the centre of the ceiling was £27; a solid old bronze Dutch candelabra. The curtains arrived as a bale of purple velour. People thought we were spending lots of money on all these things, but in actual fact none of it came out of the treasury. The Lord provided all these things; even the wallpaper. The wallpaper was 12 shillings and 6 pence a roll (62 pence in today's money). We had much criticism about spending what people thought to be a lot of money on this wallpaper, but today, 56 years later, the wallpaper is still there! Thus the library was completed and ready for the wedding! There is hardly a piece of furniture or a picture that did not come miraculously. Each piece had a history!

The "Cornfield" by John Constable

The "Cornfield" by John Constable, which hangs in the library, also had an extraordinary story. Mr. Arnell, who used to rent the warehouse in the bombed-out arcade, originally obtained this Constable. He always looked upon us as his lucky mascot when we met in the Astor Club. He always said, "Since you people moved above me, God has blessed my business." It is true that the Lord did bless Mr. Arnell. He said, "I will keep that 'Cornfield' for you. No one else is going to get it." Three years later he moved to other premises on Kew Road, since the old arcade was destroyed, and Mark's and Spencer's was built on it. I went to see him. "Where is that old Constable?" I said. "Did you really keep it for us?" "Of course I did, how dare you doubt me! It is behind that great big Victorian sideboard. I have had dealers from all over the country after that, and I shoved it behind that sideboard. You can still have it for the price I said you could, £10." On that occasion it was given to me for my birthday and I hung it in the library!

The Furnishing for the Rest of the House

Indeed, it was amazing to us how the Lord brought all the furniture and furnishings to the rest of the house. The old oil paintings, of which the "Monarch of the Glen" was among them, was 4 shillings and 6 pence (30 pence in today's money), and the "River Hepsey" in South Wales was 10 shillings (50 pence);

and many others. Much of the furniture that came to us was Georgian or Regency in keeping with the age of the property.

Lady Ogle and the Furniture

On one occasion Lady Ogle phoned us. It was a great surprise to hear her say that she was selling the great property where she lived in Oxted. She said that there were a number of items that could be useful to us and would I like to come down and view them. When I arrived at the railway station, I was met by Lady Ogle's chauffeur and driven to her home. When I arrived, she said, "I am sure you will see many pieces of furniture that will be of use to you at Halford House." The result was that we received a gift of a number of beds and day beds, chests of drawers and oil paintings. Lady Ogle, as we were going around the house, waved her hand at a cabinet and said, "Of course you will want that." I thought it was a reproduction piece, but it turned out that it was an original William and Mary cabinet from 1680 in mint condition. Even the finials and the glass were original and undamaged. It was overwhelming and I could only praise the Lord.

The Swing Chairs

However, the one gift that rendered me speechless was the gift of a swing chair. We had two dear sisters who had been staying with us from Denmark, Anna Micklesen and Sophia Jørgensen. Sophia had spent quite a large part of her life in China and had been greatly helped and influenced by Watchman Nee. They were Trojan prayer warriors. They were sitting in the garden on uncomfortable wooden chairs. I said to Margaret, who looked after the house, "I wish we had a garden swing chair, so that they could sit comfortably in the garden." Margaret said, "Oh, swing chairs are terribly expensive, but we could ask the Lord." I remembered that C.T. Studd once said, "Why ask the Lord for an egg if you can ask Him for an elephant!" So I thought to myself, should we ask for a swing chair?!

It was during a little time of prayer that we were having in Halford House when I asked the Lord for it. I had mentioned how nice it would be if we had a swing chair for the garden, but no one took it up in prayer. So I said, "Lord, if you see it as a necessity give us a swing chair!" There was a brother with us who did not believe in any sort of luxury at all, not of any kind, especially when it came to the Lord's people. We should be Spartan and utilitarian. He said, "I cannot believe the Lord would give us the luxury of a swing chair."

Three months went by and nothing happened, and I came to the conclusion that it was a luxury and that the Lord did not supply swing chairs! When I went down to Lady Ogle and got out of the car at her home she said, "Take a cup of tea with me." As we were going to this beautiful swing chair she said, "Would you like this swing chair?" Of all the gifts we received that day this one was for me the most remarkable. The other gifts were far more valuable, but the swing chair seemed to have a special message from the Lord. I could not wait to get back to Halford House to tell them that the Lord had provided the swing chair. I arrived back and told them the whole story.

The next day I was paying a visit to Mr. Ellis at his bargain shop. A great furniture van was unloading all kinds of things into the shop. In fact, a double mattress had fallen on a lady in the cellar and they were pulling her out from under it. As I was talking to Mr Ellis, at the top of the stairs, two men came in with a swing chair; they were half in and half out of the shop. "Where are we going to put this swing chair?" they asked. The shop was simply jam packed. Mr. Ellis pushed his hat back on his head and said, "Mr. Lambert, do you want a swing chair?"

"Are you giving it to me," I said.

"No," he said. "It will cost you £4."

I said, "That is a gift; we will take it."

So Mr. Ellis said to the men: "Put it back on the van and take it up to Halford House." Now we had two swing chairs!

At Halford House the next morning we were all laughing about this story and saying, "How wonderful the Lord is, and what humour the Lord has," when there was a phone call. I answered it and a terribly posh voice said, "This is Harrods. Is the leader of the Christian Fellowship a Mr. L. T. Lambert?"

"Yes," I said, "This is he speaking."

"Oh," she said, "thank you. Is the address of the Christian fellowship in Richmond, Halford House, Halford Road, Richmond, Surrey?"

"Yes," I said.

"Thank you very much; I am sorry to bother you," she said.

"Just wait," I exclaimed. "What is this all about?"

"Oh," she said, "don't you know? We have a client who has a swing chair, but she decided not to have it recovered. When we asked what we should do with the swing chair she said, 'There is a good work in Richmond led by a Mr. L. T. Lambert at Halford house,' and she was sure he would be glad to have it." Within

48 hours we had three swing chairs and had to give one of them away! No one can ever tell me that the Lord does not have great humour!

The Broadwood Grand Piano in the Main Room

We had an extraordinary old gentleman who was a piano tuner, but he was very eccentric. He was a lovable man but very solemn. He tuned our pianos. It did not matter if it was the most cherished thing you had, he was incredibly honest, direct and straight. He would tell you that what he was tuning was absolute rubbish. In fact, he had told us that the piano he tuned in our downstairs main room was rubbish; it was alright he said for young people to bang out tunes on, but he thought it was a waste of money even to tune it.

Suddenly, one day he said, "Mr. Lambert, I have been tuning a piano for some years in Isleworth, which I feel would be much better here in this place. I have been asked by the gentleman who has it if you would be interested in having it. I do not think I can tell you any more beyond that." He was an old fashioned kind of gentleman. "I cannot break any confidences," he said, "but it came from one of the highest families in the country. It is an old piano, but on this occasion I can tell you it will be very suitable for you. They only want £30 for it." I said, "Could we go and see it?" "Yes," he replied and gave me the address, so we went to see it.

The piano was originally made for Edward Cassell and his brother. They were uncles to Lady Edwina, Countess Mountbatten, the wife of Louis, Earl Mountbatten. Louis, Earl Mountbatten was Uncle to Queen Elizabeth and Prince Phillip. The gift of the piano by Edward Cassell and his brother was to Lady Edwina on her 21st birthday. The whole Cassell family were Jewish. When Lady Edwina suddenly died in Singapore, the piano was left to her butler, who now had it in the front room of his small home in Isleworth. In fact, it took up two thirds of the room. He did not really want it to go; it was his wife who wanted it out of the house. He said that if he thought it was going to a good home, he would be very happy. That is how the Broadwood Grand Piano, built like a harpsichord and with full inlaid marquetry, came to us for £30.

The Provision of Flowers

The miracles which we saw at Halford House covered every aspect of our life as a fellowship of God's people. I remember one occasion in the early days when I was in the house one Friday, working alone and sitting in the study, I left the study and went across the main downstairs room to do something. Suddenly, I realised we had no flowers for the weekend meetings. I remember thinking, this is the first time in our history we have not had any flowers for the weekend, nor a penny with which to buy them. My sister, who was fully trained in floral arrangement, used to do them. "Well, that is it," I thought to myself and went back into the study and continued working.

Suddenly there was a ring at the front door and I went over and opened it. There was a mammoth black limousine parked in front of the door. Standing before me was a chauffeur dressed in a black suit, with an enormous bunch of flowers in his arms. He said, "These are for you, sir."

I said, "You have got it wrong; you want Professor Hullah Brown next door."

He said, "Aren't you the Christian Fellowship?"

I said that we were, and he put them in my arms. "Thank you very much," I said, and shut the door. I had asked him where they came from but all he said was that they were an anonymous gift from the North. Did he drive all the way from the North with that bunch of flowers? We will never know. I have never seen that car or the chauffeur since. Some thought it was Lady Ogle's car and chauffeur, but it was not. It dawned on me that the Lord had provided the flowers, and I praised Him.

At about 2 o'clock there was another ring at the door. I went to open it and there was a big green Interflora van, and the man said, "For the Christian Fellowship from Liverpool." We did not know anybody in Liverpool. I took the flowers and asked, "Who are these people from Liverpool." He said, "Anonymous, sir." I signed the receipt and he drove off. We had so many flowers that weekend we did not know what to do with them all. It seemed to me to be so funny that the one weekend we had no money for flowers that so many flowers came to us.

The Lady from the Marriage Guidance Council

On one occasion there was a ring at the front door and Margaret went to answer it. It was a lady from the marriage guidance council. She had heard of the fellowship and wanted to find out what it was and what it did. Margaret invited her in and began to answer her questions. One of the questions she asked was how we were financed. Margaret explained to her that none of us took wages but trusted in God; and that we did not have collections or make appeals or make our financial needs known, but we trusted in God. Margaret had witnessed to her how the Lord miraculously met all our needs.

The lady was impressed and said that she had read the story of the small woman with a big heart and great faith, Gladys Aylward of China. As they were talking in the hallway of Halford House, there was a little rattle at the front door. There in the small letterbox was a roll of bank notes, half in and half out. "Oh," Margaret said, "I think this is the money we have been praying for." She took it out and counted it. It was indeed the exact sum.

The lady from the marriage guidance council nearly fainted and was so impacted that she had to sit down. "I have heard of things like this, but have never seen it with my own eyes," she said. She then got up and thanking Margaret she went out through the front door. However, she felt so faint from the shock that she felt she could not get on her bicycle lest she fall off.

One of the sisters in the fellowship, who happened to know her, met her pushing her bicycle up Richmond Hill. When they greeted each other, this lady told Myrtle Payne, "I am still in a state of shock and could not trust myself on a bicycle! I had heard of how God meets the needs of those who trust Him, but had never seen it happen until now. I saw God meet some need just now in Halford House." "That happens all the time there," said Myrtle.

4.
God's Special Gift to Us

The Advent of Bill Richards

When God gave us Bill Richards, it signaled a new phase in the recovery and reconstruction of Halford House. Bill was a Cockney, a hugely strong man; his arms were the size of my legs. There was nothing he could not turn his hand to in building and reconstruction and renovation. He was always cheerful and had a very positive attitude toward life and work. He believed that with every problem there was always a way through!

I first met him in the residential part of the house in the apartment of Professor Hullah Brown. He was taking out all the wood-boring beetle and dry rot damage in their living quarters. Hilda, Hullah Brown's wife, said to me: "You must meet Bill. He is a remarkably clever carpenter and builder." Hullah Brown had been playing the piano in their lounge whilst Hilda was listening to him. Their maid of many years was knitting and the ancient dog and cat were resting, whilst the hen was perched on the back of the settee. Suddenly, Hullah Brown disappeared as the floor gave way. He slowly went down, still playing, until he reached the earth, a full meter below the floor! The dry rot and wood-boring beetles had done their work. It was rather like the organs in old cinemas which used to be played in the interval. They used to ascend and then gradually descend whilst someone played them. Bill Richards was employed by the Hullah's to replace the timbers and give them a good, new strong floor.

The Hiring of Bill

Bill was a genius with anything to do with wood as well as building. We were not satisfied with the firm that did the initial and basic restoration. Some of the work they had done was cosmetic. I spoke to Bill and told him what we needed. He responded very favourably. I then felt that I should be absolutely honest about our finances. I told him we were nearly all young people and most of us were students. There were few large wage earners amongst us, if any! If he worked for us I told him it would be as if God was employing him. He needed to be very precise and accurate in his work and God would meet the financial needs.

Bill said that he did not believe in God, but respected those who did. I said, "Are you ready to do all this work knowing our financial background?" He said, "Yeah, no problem!" Years later he told me: "I did not believe what you said. I looked at you, then I looked at the house, and I thought: they have money, and they have it in the bank; it is just the way Christians talk. They say they have no money and that they trust God, and then they go down to the bank, take it out and give it to me."

God Meeting Bill's Expenses

It must have seemed like that to Bill, for every time he asked for a sum of money for the many and different expenses incurred relating to the restoration and renovation, it was provided. Over the years Bill would come each week with the expenses of the timber and other items, as well as his work, and every single time the Lord miraculously met those needs—sometimes in extraordinary ways. It was natural for Bill to believe that we were going down to the bank and taking out the money. He did not believe that we actually got on our knees and sought the Lord to meet those needs. Sometimes it was £200, other times it was a £100, or £75 and many other large or small sums. Over the years the Lord met all those weekly needs. As a fellowship of believers we learnt so much of the Lord's ways—His faithfulness, His love, His mercy, and we grew by His grace. Bill had all his needs met, and continued in his agnosticism.

The Gift of £300

Then came the occasion when we needed £300 on a Thursday morning. Bill came to me at about 10 o'clock. He had now learnt our phraseology: "Has the money come?" he said.

"No," I said, "it has not!"

He looked at me very strangely and then said: "Will it come?"

I said, "Have you done the job properly?"

"Oh yeah, well maybe a screw here and a screw there."

I said, "See that the screw here and there is put in, because I am quite sure God will meet the need. By what time do you have to have the money?"

"Two o'clock," he said, "to get it into the bank by 3 o'clock."

Then I said, "It will be here by 2 o'clock."

"Oh," he said, "I am so glad;" and he went out thinking I had forgotten to go to the bank. In fact we had no money! The first mail came and no money; the second post came with only bills. There were altogether thirteen of us Christians around the house and garden that day, and I remember saying, "Let us have an early lunch and we will go into the library and pray for this money to come."

So we all gathered in the library, shut the door, and in a big circle got on our knees. Bill came through the back door, looked in the kitchen and there was no one there. Then he went into the main room and likewise there was no one there. He went across the main room to my study, looked through the glass door, and no one was there. He heard voices and realised they were coming from the library. He walked past the inside of the front door and went up the stairs and quietly opened the library door. To his amazement he saw thirteen people on their knees in a big circle and heard Albert Luck praying, "Lord, we ain't got this £300 and it is 2 o'clock and we need it right now within the next ten minutes!" Of course, Bill shut the door. I had heard the door open and I heard an awful sigh from Bill as he shut the door. I heard another great groan and a thumping noise as he went down the stairs like a drunk man, saying loudly, "Oh Gawd, they ain't got no money; they are praying for it." On the door mat at the bottom of the stairs over which he had just come a minute before was a pile of three hundred £1 notes. He scooped up this great mass of notes, and making a terrific noise as he came up the stairs, he opened the door, interrupting our prayer, saying, "You can all stop praying; the money has come!"

It was three hundred £1 notes. To this day we do not know how it happened because Bill had passed by that door only a few moments before. Did someone stand outside the front door flicking through a very small letterbox three hundred £1 notes? Then again, whoever gave the money had faith because any of the other workmen could have come in and taken it. Of course, it may have been the Lord Himself who manufactured the notes! Nevertheless, Bill became a believer in God. However it came about, it was the Lord who did it!

The £100 from the Herbrides

On another occasion Bill came late one Wednesday evening at about 7 o'clock and said to me: " 'Ere, Lance, I forgot to tell you earlier I need £100 for timber tomorrow morning."

"Bill," I said, "fancy coming so late; what do you expect us to do at this time? You should have told us earlier."

"Oh," he said, "but I thought you prayed."

"Of course we pray," I said, "but we do not have a prayer meeting tonight."

I had wondered whether there was someone wealthy amongst us who knew of the needs and then gave the money. It was an evil heart of unbelief in me. Now it really had to be the Lord. I went back home and said to the Lord: "I am the only one along with Bill who knows about this need of £100." The next morning as I came into Halford House I swear I almost heard a divine chuckle. There were three envelopes, two were bills and the third letter was from the Hebrides, posted three days before. In it was a cheque dated four days before for £100. The letter said: "I have had your fellowship on my heart for three weeks and I cannot get it off. The only way I can do it is by giving you this cheque. I do not know what it is for, but you must surely know." I did know and praised the Lord; and Bill got his £100.

The £1000 and the Tea Caddy Full of Money

I was sitting in the library one day and there were some letters which had come. I opened one of them and took out a cheque. I really thought I had lost my sight. I kept on looking at it because it was a cheque that seemed to be for £1000. We had never before had a gift for that amount. I kept on looking at it and thought it must be only for £100. Then I called Ivy, who was in the kitchen and she said, "Yes." So I said, "Come up here quickly." She came belting up the stairs. Showing her the cheque, I said, "Look at that. I think I am seeing double; does it say 100 or 1000?" She said it was a 1000! "Well," I said, "Look at this letter." It was a letter from a bank manager from a place down in the South of England. It simply said, "A client of ours wishes to make this gift of money to you anonymously in connection with building work." We could only praise the Lord. I said to Ivy, "We have never had a gift like this before. I feel weak around the knees; let's have a cup of tea." "Yes," she said. She belted back down the stairs and put on the kettle. Then I heard a piercing shriek and quickly went down. I thought to myself as I went down, it is probably a mouse that she has seen. At this point Ivy was coming up the stairs with the tea caddy, and she said: "Look." There in the tea caddy were pound notes. We went everywhere through the whole house looking under cushions to see if there were anymore!

The Faith Position of Halford House

It would be good at this point in the record to explain our attitude to financing. At the beginning of the history of the fellowship we had the normal kind of collections in our meetings. It was the usual evangelical practice of collecting and raising money which we followed. On one occasion early on we had a discussion around Matthew chapter 6:3—4: "But when thou doest alms, let not thy left hand know what thy right hand doeth: that thine alms may be in secret: and thy Father who seeth in secret shall recompense thee."

The result of our fellowship over this led us to the conclusion that advertising our needs or collecting money in meetings was not honouring to the Lord. After all, in a collection your left hand certainly knows what your right hand is doing, and so does everybody else! It is a public act. If we are to give in secret there must be another manner in which to give our gifts. Collections were not *thine alms may be in secret*. There is nothing secret about a collection. The same could be said of appealing for money and advertising the needs.

We therefore concluded that we should have a treasury built in wood and placed somewhere in the house. To give would then be a personal act of worship seen only by God. We taught that everybody should know the blessing of giving, that we should always give more than the tithe that was necessary under the Old Covenant.

From the day that we made this decision, we never had another collection or advertised our financial needs outside of a prayer meeting. The incredible story of God's provision must surely have something to do with this position of faith.

The treasury was divided into three sections. The first section was designated for the work of the Lord centred in Halford House; the second section was for the workers, those either in the ministry of His Word or in practical serving; and the third section was for those in social need. Anything that was specifically designated had to be used for the purpose it was given. From the first two sections we tithed what was given and placed it in the third for social needs. None of the workers at Halford House received wages including myself. Although we were entitled biblically to wages, we believed that there was a higher level by not taking them, and we would have a greater reward in the kingdom (see I Timothy 5:17—18 cp. I Corinthians 9:18; II Corinthians 11:7).

It is once again an amazing fact that the first weekend we adopted this position the giving in the fellowship trebled and has never gone back to a poorer level.

I remember a very well known and Godly leader in the evangelical world contacting me over this matter and expressing how concerned he was about the financial position we were taking. He said, "Unless the Lord's people see a collection plate they will never be reminded to give and you will end up starving." I can only say that I am thankful we never left that position and the testimony of Halford House is its confirmation.

Insurance–to Have or Not to Have

The question of whether we should insure the work of reconstruction and renovation, as well as the home itself with all the items that were in it, was the cause of much discussion. One or two of the business people amongst us were seriously bothered that we were not insured. Whenever the matter came up they raised the possibility of unsaved workmen harming themselves or seriously being wounded whilst on the site. They said, "We could be sued by their families." Even outside the fellowship there were those who were sympathetic to us who advised us to be insured. I remember one man who said, "Lance, promise you will have this place insured. You cannot have a place like this, with all these valuable things and not be insured. You must be insured!" On another occasion someone said, "What would happen if Bill Richards had a serious accident? Who is going to pay for it?"

We were not against insuring our homes or businesses or taking out life insurance, but we felt that it was a personal matter between a believer and God. Storms and troubles come on both the righteous and the unrighteous. I had a friend in the United States who, by mistake, insured his beach home three times with different insurance companies. How he managed to do that I do not know! However, when this huge hurricane hit the Gulf of Mexico it destroyed his whole beach home. The only thing they found was one bidet! He, however, was able to claim the total cost three times over!

The problem we had as a fellowship of believers was that Halford House was a gift from God, and He made it very clear that it represented Him. It was something that God was reconstructing and renovating. To take out insurance seemed to be an insurance against any failures the Lord might make!! Interestingly, we all felt the same including those brothers who originally had questions.

We took this whole matter to the Lord in prayer and asked Him to speak to us and we got an incredible reply: "Some trust in chariots, and some in horses; but we will make mention of the name of the Lord our God." (Psalm 20:7). We never took out the insurance but trusted God.

Bill Falls from the Top of the Roof in the Main Room

On one occasion I needed to see Bill, and I knew he was working on the roof of the large main upstairs meeting room. To my surprise, as I went up the fire escape I saw a young man who was dressed like a Teddy boy (an older form of punk rocker), looking a bit white. We had prayed for him. He worked at the shop on the corner of Halford Road. As I reached the top of the fire escape, he was leaning on the door which was open, smoking a cigarette. I said, "Hello," and asked whether Bill was there.

"Yes," he said, "he is in there."

He then went on to say, " 'Ere, do you believe in miracles?"

I was a little taken aback, but I quickly recovered and said, "Actually I do!"

Then he replied, "Well I have just seen one!"

And then a voice inside the room said, "Yeah, so have I." It was Bill.

I had noticed that Bill was sitting on a chair in the middle of 200 wheel-back chairs which did not belong to us; we were storing them for someone else. They were all piled up one on top of the other with their legs sticking up. Right in the middle of this jam packed pile of chairs was one chair that did not have another chair on top of it. There was no way in and no way out. Bill was sitting on that chair. I thought to myself, "How strange that he is sitting in a chair right in the middle of them! Has he climbed over those chairs to sit in that one chair? Why did he not pull out one of the outside chairs and sit down on it?"

Then the Teddy boy said, "I came into this big room and there was no ceiling here, only rafters. I called up, 'Bill!'"

And Bill said, "Yes!"

"It is so and so," I said, "and I want to speak with you."

Bill said, "I will come down." Bill let himself down through the opening and his legs were trying to find the ladder forgetting he had pulled it up onto the outer roof. He had let himself down too far to pull himself back up.

The Teddy boy said, "Bill fell but he did not fall normally; he floated down, somersaulted, and landed in that chair where he has been sitting ever since."

Bill said, "Yeah, I came down like a fevver (feather)."

He was unharmed, unbruised, and within minutes of talking with his friend had gone back to the work on the roof.

Bill Falls from the Chimney of the Residential House

Margaret, who cared for the whole house, and I, were having a midmorning cup of tea in the study. Suddenly there was the most fearful thump and the whole house, with its 17 rooms, shook. I exclaimed, "Whatever was that?" Margaret immediately said, "Bill has probably thrown something down from the roof next door. He is working on the chimneys." These chimneys towered well above the roof of the manor house. You could say that it was the equivalent of at least four floors.

As Margaret said these words, there was a piercing scream from next door. It came from Eunice, a fully qualified nurse, who was visiting Blanche. When this huge thump shook the whole house, Blanche had said to Eunice, "Go and see what that is." Eunice had gone to the bedroom window, looked down, and saw Bill spread-eagled on the concrete. He had fallen the equivalent of four floors, and his weight had shaken the whole house. Naturally she screamed, for she thought he was dead.

When Margaret and I heard the scream, we jumped up and quickly walked around the house and met Blanche and Eunice coming from the other direction. Bill was still spread-eagled on the concrete. I was sure he was dead, but he began to move and slowly got up. I had heard of cases where people, who were dead, had spontaneously moved from nervous reaction. Bill, however, said, "I am quite all right. I have no broken bones and no bruises;" and to show this he began moving his arms and legs up and down. I said to Blanche and Eunice: "Get him a chair."

Whilst he sat there Blanche and Eunice made him a cup of tea. Eunice said to Blanche, "He needs something more than tea; have you got any brandy?" "No," Blanche said, "I have not, but I do have some very expensive whiskey which Ivan (her husband) had stored." They poured a dram of whiskey into the tea. Eunice said, "Don't tell Lance." However, I had noticed that Bill drank immediately three cups of tea, one after the other! He then got up and said that he would continue working. I insisted that he should see a doctor. He refused. I then insisted that he go home and rest which he did. He was back the next morning ready to work. He had not suffered a single bruise, ache or problem as a result of his fall.

I only found out about the whiskey in the tea many years later at the 50th anniversary of Halford House when Eunice and Blanche finally confessed what they had done! I still chuckle about it today.

Bill and His Steering Wheel

The only time I ever saw Bill unnerved, shocked and unable to work, was the occasion when he drove up to Richmond from beyond Godalming where he lived, a distance of at least 22 miles (34 kilometres). He used to do this every day at great speed in just over half an hour. He loved to drive fast. He arrived at Halford House and was parking outside the front door when the steering wheel came away in his hand. He realised then that if it had happened on the journey when he was speeding, he would have been dead. He was so shaken that he could not work and had to take the day off.

These three stories reveal the faithfulness of the Lord. As a fellowship we had taken a position of absolute trust in the Lord based on the word He had given us. He had not failed us.

The Brick Crisis

The building inspector on one occasion, when he was inspecting everything at the house, informed us that he did not believe that the south-western brick wall was strong enough to carry the number of people that would meet in the upper main meeting room. He insisted that the wall had to come down and be rebuilt. We had discovered that he was a Christian. He said, "After all, if Billy Graham came to speak the place would be jam packed, and we have to make provision for such an event." So the wall was demolished. It required a new much stronger foundation and then the rebuilding of the whole wall.

The Drought from April to September

We then had to pray for a drought for the duration of the wall being down. Bill had said to us that when this whole wall is down, we will have tarpaulins hanging from the roof right down to the ground. If we have big storms it could get very wet inside and we will not be able to work properly to get it done. So we got on our knees and asked the Lord to give us good dry weather.

From April until September, amazingly for Britain, we did not have a drop of rain on the garden. It had to be hosed. Some of us actually stood and watched huge thunderstorms and cloud bursts in Richmond Park and over Wimbledon and Kingston, but not on us. Bill used to say, "You wait: when you see the great bow windows go into the rebuilt wall, it will come down like 'cats and dogs.'" When the windows went in, it came down like a cloudburst just as Bill had said. It was unforgettable.

The Yellow Stock Bricks

The building inspector came and said to Bill: "I hope you are building this wall in old yellow stocks? This is a classified building and you are not permitted to use new bricks." Bill had a fit. To find these bricks he spent days phoning all over the South of England from Bath to Exeter but could not find any. Finally, he found these old yellow stock bricks, unbelievably in Putney, a short bus or train ride from Richmond. While we were having the Bible study downstairs the bricks were being delivered outside the windows. The wall was completed and we praised the Lord.

Bill and the RSJ's

Another miracle of the first order was the RSJ's (Rolled Steel Joists) that we needed. They had to be some thirty-two feet long and more than three feet in depth. They had to span the width of the main upstairs meeting room and had to be specially made for this house. We ordered them a month or two before and they were brought down by an enormous trailer. I can never forget it because they could hardly get them up Halford Road. Finally, they managed and these two huge RSJ's were placed alongside the rebuilt wall.

Bill then asked Mowlems, one of the biggest crane firms in the country, if they could take over the job of swinging these two RSJ's over the Red Cross Hut (which was next door) and into their position on the two pillars which he had built for them. An eighty-foot jig crane needed to be in Halford Road to swing these RSJ's into their position. As a result the police were going to close Halford Road for a whole day. The reason we had to have such a huge crane was due to the protected Yew tree, which was in the garden, and the Red Cross Hut—both of them being in the way. Bill had an intuition that something would go wrong, but the company assured him that they did this kind of work all the time and never had any trouble.

However, he persisted, and finally they sent a man down to inspect it. He took one look at the yew tree and the Red Cross hut and the other two roofs, over which the crane had to swing the RSJ's, and said, "There is no go! We cannot possibly allow you to have the crane; it would be far too big a risk. As we swing it over, if one of those girders were to get into "a swing," it would crush that hut completely." Thus, at the last moment Mowlems pulled out!

Bill was nonplussed. He had gotten everything ready for the next day. He had tarpaulins over the roof in case the weather became bad. Now it seemed that he had the roof off and could do nothing about it. We said that we would pray about it. Then after a little while he came back and said: "You know, I believe we can do it. I am going to get it up the way the Pyramids were built, with block and tackle."

The problem was that Bill was the only man on the job. Then he managed to get another man to help, an engineer who had mostly been building ships. Bill said, "He will help I am sure." I can never forget that day—those Douglas fir beams, like huge trunks on one side of the house, and then two or three more Douglas fir beams all bound together with a block and pulley on the other side. Bill inched up one RSJ after the other. It was an inch at a time. The engineer who was helping him was terrified. I have never seen a man so terrified in my life; he was pouring with perspiration on a reasonably cool day. Bill said afterwards, "I would rather have done it all alone."

At the same time, since there was no one else, Margaret and I were involved. Bill had said that normally when you do it in this old fashioned way there has to be someone on either end of the RSJ steadying it so that it does not swing up and down. He said the way to do it is to put a coil around the beam and tie it around the waist of each person. Margaret tied it around her waist and held it there. She was at one end and I was at the other end with it tied around my waist. Slowly it went up inch by inch as we gradually let out the coil. Then the phone rang and I did not think properly. I just thought, "Oh, the phone, the phone." I dropped the rope and went in to answer it. All I remember was seeing Margaret going up into the air and saying at the top of her voice, "Lance, get back!"

The amazing fact was that those two RSJ's were an absolutely perfect fit. Bill had said to us as we were having a cup of tea: "The one thing I am frightened about is that those RSJs will not go in properly. I could not lift them, and without the crane there is no possibility of fiddling around with them and getting them right. It is going to be a miracle if they just go in exactly in the right position." That is precisely what happened; it was the Lord. We had saved a lot of money by not having to hire the crane and close the road for the day. The only thing we did not lose was the Red Cross Hut; that was still with us! Only those who were part of the story at the time will understand. The Red Cross Hut was a First World War Hut which had been placed on our ground and over which we had many battles!

Once again we had proved the absolute reliability and faithfulness of the Lord to His Word and to those He saves. It is no small matter to trust the Lord with all your heart, and to lean not on your own understanding.

5.
The Completion of the Main Upstairs Meeting Room

The Hullah Brown's Roof

By the grace of God we had now come to the reconstruction and renovation of the main upstairs meeting room. At that time we were comfortably filling the downstairs meeting room. God had kept us reasonably small through all those years because He was doing a work in us. He had indeed moulded us as a prayer instrument in His hand. On one occasion, He even said in a prophetic utterance that He would keep us small but hone us as an instrument of intercession.

Nevertheless, there was a sense in the fellowship that the time had come to complete the main upstairs room, and we made the decision together to go ahead. We had in hand £450 to be spent on the upstairs. It was interesting that we always seemed to be dealing with sums of £450!

At the very point when we made the decision, Mrs. Hullah Brown came round and did what she always did, tapped on the study window, and I opened it. She was a dear soul and on this occasion she said, "I have bad news. Something has to be done about the roof next door. Water is pouring in on all our possessions." I used to say to her whenever she implied expenditures were necessary for her side of the house: "But Mrs. Hullah, what can we do? We only receive £1.50 in rent from you for the whole house." Nevertheless, I believed the righteous thing to do was to get Bill Richards to have a look at it, which he did. Well, he came back to me and said, "It will cost £450, because every tile on the roof is a handmade tile and has got to be replaced exactly as it is." I thought to myself: if we go on with this work that will be the £450 to start the renovation work on the upstairs room and it will be wiped out.

As a fellowship of believers we sought the Lord for His direction. There was not a little discussion about this situation. It was natural that some of us, with good business minds, could not understand why we should give up the £450 we had in our possession for the upstairs meeting room when the Hullah Browns only paid £1.50 a week. One brother said, "Let the water go in; otherwise you are going to have them in there forever! She is twenty years younger than him and when he is gone, she will be there for another twenty years. You will never get practically into the possession of that house." Others felt we should pay for their roof and trust the Lord. After much prayer and less discussion we all became convinced that the right action to take was to rebuild the roof next door and trust the Lord for the main upstairs meeting room.

The Cheque from Glasgow

The very next day there was a letter from Glasgow, and in it was a cheque for £500. The giver wrote, "We do not quite know what you are doing; but here is a gift for it." The interesting fact is that we had made a decision that every gift that came for the material and physical rebuilding should be tithed and the tithe put towards people in need. So the gift of £500 was the £450 for the next door roof and the £50 tithe! It was a marvellous confirmation from the Lord that we were doing the right thing, both in rebuilding the Hullah's roof and tithing everything from the physical reconstruction for people in need.

The result of our taking responsibility for the roof next door meant that our relationship with the Hullah Browns became very loving. They used to say that until we all came on the scene they had lost faith in the new generation. On the human level it was quite normal that people should have questions about taking the money we had for the upstairs room and using it instead for next door. The Lord enabled us to do the righteous thing, and when the time came for the whole residential house to be used by the fellowship, it came to pass without argument, rancour, or bitterness.

The Miracle of the Vanished Main Beam

It was somewhere around this time when we had decided that the Lord wanted us to go ahead with the upstairs main meeting room, that Bill came down to the study and said to me, "You had better come up and look at this." When I went up the stairs, the first thing I saw were Bill's workers, some of them quite old, standing and looking up as if they were seeing a vision. Some of them had even taken their caps off. The huge main beam, upon which rested the roof of the library and the roof of the main upstairs meeting room, had disappeared. This main beam was originally from a ship wreck. Dry rot and wood boring beetles had reduced it to powder. The two roofs were resting on nothing! At times there had been heavy snowfalls and it was remarkable that the two roofs had stayed up. To Bill and the workmen, as well as ourselves, it was a complete miracle.

The Entrance to the Main Upstairs Room, the Stairs and Landing

When the stairs were renewed which led up to the main upstairs meeting room and to the library, we discovered another miracle. Many times at Christmas we had Carol services and parties. During those times some folks came to the Lord. At many of those especial meeting times the library was full to the brim and people sat outside on the landing and down the stairs.

When the time came to reconstruct the upper main room, to our total surprise we discovered that the landing and stairs were resting on nothing. It was miraculous that we had never had a serious accident. The whole landing and everyone on it could have totally collapsed, with disastrous results for all. Bill thought that the angels must have been working overtime!

The Installation of Central Heating for the Whole Property

Great Britain had a great freeze in the winter of 1962–1963. All those of us who were alive at that time will remember it. It started snowing during the Boxing Day party on the 26th December and the snow never left our lawn until the end of April and the beginning of May of 1963. In that one winter we spent a fortune on keeping the place warm. If once we had burst pipes we knew that dry rot would start up again, as well as the mould that could also result. We had to have log fires in the rooms in which there were fire places, electric hot air convectors, electric radiators, and paraffin oil stoves in the other rooms. Even then we felt frozen. It was Ralph Hardie who said: "Well, of course, you will always feel cold until you have a proper heating system for the whole house; not only for this side but also for next door." It was worked out that with full central heating we would spend the same amount for the whole property as we had spent on keeping two or three rooms half warm. We also would not have the risk of frozen pipes and all the other potential problems, such as dry rot and mould, etc.

Now the obstacle to moving ahead was the capital outlay. We knew that the running costs would be low. It was the financial sum which we would need to install a proper central heating system that was the concern. Would the Lord have us trust Him for that sum? With the old way of trying to heat the rooms, condensation ran down the walls in rivers. It was so bad that sometimes people thought we had leaking pipes.

A Miracle of the First Order

When we asked a company that installed central heating to give us a quote, we were told by them that they could not do it under £2400. We then sought the Lord, and we all felt that we should go ahead. He met all the costs of the installation throughout the latter part of 1963. In the late winter or early spring of 1964 we had the last sum to pay, £348. It was amazing that all the other large costs were met, but this last sum obstinately remained. Naturally we began to ask what could be wrong.

Suddenly, in a prayer meeting in the library one day the Lord flashed into my heart, "Faith has to be concretely expressed." Again and again in the story of Halford House we had expressed our faith in words to Bill or to the others involved in the reconstruction work that the Lord would supply the financial need and He did. With this large heating installation company there had been no opportunity to express such faith. They had no idea about our having to trust the Lord. Each time they needed a sum, it came. Then I wondered whether we should send the cheque for the £348. I did not know at the time that it was illegal to send a cheque if you did not have the funds in the account; it is, however, obvious that such an action would be wrong. I do not advocate this kind of action, but we thought it was the way the Lord was leading us.

After the cheque was made out by the brother who looked after the treasury and was also a tax officer, someone else signed it. Then it was awaiting my countersignature. I countersigned it and decided to wait until the next morning to see if the Lord would send something in the mail, or by another means that would clear the bill. However nothing came! What did come was a phone call from the managing director of the heating installation company. He said, "Oh, Mr. Lambert, I have just phoned to ask how you are."

I said, "I am very well, thank you very much."

He said, "Are you nice and warm?"

I said, "Oh, yes. We are enjoying the central heating. We have never known such warmth in this house, and we have no condensation. We can go into any of the rooms and feel warm. It is really wonderful."

"Well," he said, "I am so glad. You have got no complaints about the way the work was done?"

I said, "None at all! In fact we were very pleased about the cleanliness of the men, their speed and efficiency; they were marvellous."

"Oh, well, that is all I wanted to know," he said. "Will the little outstanding amount be coming? We need it badly. Would you put it in the post straight away?"

"Yes," I said and thought, "Lord, you have to do it now." So I posted the cheque immediately.

Two weeks went by and David Hilditch (the brother who took care of the treasury) came to me and said, "Do you think I should go to the bank manager? He has not gotten in touch with me. We must be £348 in the red! We have never been in the red before you know. That is quite a bit of money to be in the red." However, I did not feel he should go and see the bank manager. I had said there is an old saying, "Let sleeping dogs lie." It was then that someone said to me: "It is illegal to send a cheque without having sufficient funds to honour it." Then one of our ex-borstal boys who had been saved came to me and jokingly said, "I will see you in prison." So when David next came, I said, "David, go and see the bank manager."

David went down to the bank but he did not see the bank manager. He was quite shrewd; he went up to the man at the desk and said, "Could I please have our balance sheet, our statement?" The clerk gave him the statement. The £348 was not on the statement. After a week had passed he asked again, and still it was not on the statement. David went down to the bank for the third time. On this occasion the clerk gave him the statement and it showed that someone had paid in the £348 and that it had been paid out on the same day. David said to the clerk, "I cannot understand this! It says it was paid here on such and such a date, but I have been in twice before and it was not on the statement then." "Yes," the clerk said, "the sum was paid into another branch, and because they did not understand the three accounts you have, they did not know which account to put it in; hence the non showing of the sum until now. In fact it was a slip-up on our part that you were not notified." The amazing thing is this; the needed sum of £348 was paid into that branch the very morning that the cheque for £348 was posted to the heating company. Whoever it was who paid in the £348, we do not know! Only the Lord knows! We, however, were never in the red. It was a miracle of the first order.

The Panelling for the Main Upstairs Meeting Room

One of the features of that upstairs room was the beautiful panelling in pine wood. It was the work of Bill Richards and was outstanding. Finding the right kind of wood panelling presented us with a difficult problem, especially as there was a large amount of wall to be covered. The wood specialist firm that Bill and I visited had only a certain amount of suitable wood panelling. We bought all that they had. The amazing fact was that it covered the walls exactly to the inch.

The Baptistery

One of the young brothers who had come to the Lord amongst us was an apprentice stone mason. His name was Johnnie Dyer. He asked his boss whether he could line the baptistery to be built for us with green and white marble. His boss had been very impressed with what happened to him. Johnnie was a changed man. The boss said he would love to do it, and although we would have to pay for the marble the work would be free. The result was an incredibly beautiful baptistery.

As usual it was the chief building inspector who put a spanner in the works. He said there was absolutely no way that we could build a baptistery upstairs! Did we have any idea the weight a baptistery would be when filled with water and the weight of at least two people in it as well?! It seemed that the possibility of a baptistery in the upstairs main room was impossible. Then we discovered that in the old residential part of the house, the original but defunct large fire place of the kitchen was built exactly where we wanted the baptistery. By that time the residential house had come into our full and practical possession. It provided the perfect foundation for the baptistery. Over the years many were baptised in it.

The Two Large Brass Candelabras

This is the story of the two magnificent brass candelabras which light the main upstairs meeting room. Diana Miles had died in tragic circumstances in 1974 and her parents and family wanted to give a sum of money in memory of her. They thought that the two main candelabras, giving light to the upstairs meeting room, would be a perfect way to commemorate her. An American brother also gave a sum of money to cover not only the two candelabras but all the wall lighting in keeping with them.

I remembered that there was a shop in Notting Hill that sold those kinds of lamps, but could not recall where it was or its name. I went down to Betty Redman, who owned an antique shop in Brewers Lane, and asked her if she could remember the name of the shop. She could not recall the name either, but thought it was in Notting Hill, somewhere on the left!

The Notting Hill Lamp Shop

Then I said to Paul Skaife: "Let's go and investigate." So we got into the car and just literally went. I will never forget it and neither, I suppose, will Paul. We drifted across to the Great West Road and we came to Notting Hill. Instead of going to the left we turned to the right, and almost immediately saw this shop with all these lamps. I said to Paul, "That looks like the shop I was thinking about. Even if it is not, it is worth our going in to have a look."

The proprietors in the shop were exceedingly pleasant people and very helpful. When we said what we wanted they said, "We are sure we can do something like this for you." However, the lady said, "I just wish you could wait because my nephew will be coming any moment and he deals with these kinds of things." So we decided to wait for the nephew. The nephew, a very nice youngish man, walked in, shook our hands and began talking. "Where are you from?" he said.

"Richmond," we said.

"Oh," he said, "I live in Richmond over in East Twickenham. Where are these lights for?"

We said, "Halford House."

"Halford House," he said. "So you must be believers?"

"Why, yes," we said. "So am I; my name is Michael Denton. I go to Saint Stephens and I have often prayed for you at Halford House. I am not sure if we could do a special deal on these lamps." He then showed us two solid brass Dutch style candelabras, and said, "Any thief would think that they were the originals. If they were they would be worth £200 a piece. These however were made by us."

Thus we bought the two candelabras and also a number of wall lights that were in keeping with them.

To us it was miraculous the way the Lord had led us. Out of all those shops in the Notting Hill area we were led to this believer. When we got into the car to go to the Notting Hill area, we only had the vaguest idea where this shop might be. The Lord, however, led us, and we came to the only shop where a believer, who was living in the Richmond area and was attending a living assembly, could deal with us. We considered it miraculous.

A House of the Lord for All Nations

*And it shall come to pass in the latter days, that the
mountain of the Lord's house shall be established on the
top of the mountains, and shall be exalted above the hills;
and all nations shall flow unto it. And many peoples shall
go and say, Come ye, and let us go up to the mountain
of the Lord, to the house of the God of Jacob; and he shall
teach us of his ways, and we will walk in his paths: for
out of Zion shall go forth the law, and the word of the
Lord from Jerusalem (Isaiah 2:2—3 cp Micah 4:1—2).*

At the time that the Lord gave us this Scripture, He used three
independent believers, so that what He was saying to us would
be established in the mouth of at least three witnesses. It seemed
that He was indicating that He wanted to do something special
for His use and to His glory. When this happened, I wondered
how a Scripture which was all to do with the Temple, the House
of the Lord in Jerusalem, could be applied to us in Great Britain.
After all we were a small fellowship of young believers, ostracised,
ignored and much spoken against. None of us were influential
or famous.

Since the years which have followed, it seems that the Lord was
signifying that Halford House and everything to do with it was a
sign. The house that He gave us was on Richmond Hill, albeit the
lower part of the hill. Everything to do with it, from beginning to
end, had been His work. The provision of the house, the provision
of the money, the provision of the furniture and furnishings,
all were a witness and a testimony to Him.

We never had a meeting where less than 14 nations were present. Sometimes it was 24 nations. To mention just a few of them, there were believers in the fellowship from Norway, Sweden, Denmark, Finland, Germany, the Netherlands, France, Switzerland, Italy, Greece, Singapore, Hong Kong, Indonesia, Malaysia, Mali, the former Czechoslovakia, the United States, and Canada. The Lord had said: *All nations shall flow unto it*, and in some small way it had come to pass.

Certainly we had all been taught *His ways* and led to *walk in His paths*. It had not all been light and joy. We had gone through some very real periods of testing and loss, and out of it the Lord had brought us into much spiritual wealth. One such period was from 1955 to 1957, when for three years, we seemed to suffer only loss. It was our baptism of fire. It was as if the evangelical world was totally against us. We were ostracised by all. Our fellowship with T. Austin-Sparks, with Watchman Nee, and with Bahkt Singh seemed to be the reason for it. The ministry of those brothers upset the normal evangelical world. The advent of the book, "The Normal Christian Life" by Watchman Nee began to change things.

The Place Is Too Strait for Me

Suddenly from 1965 we began to multiply. The Lord was bringing us out into a large place. In the worst of the battle, when I felt somehow responsible for the ostracism and condemnation, the Lord spoke to me one morning from Isaiah 49:14—21:

But Zion said, The Lord hath forsaken me, and the Lord hath forgotten me. Can a woman forget her sucking child, that she should not have compassion on the son of her womb? yea, these may forget, yet will not I forget thee. Behold, I have graven thee upon the palms of my hands; thy walls are continually before me. Thy children make haste; thy destroyers and they that made thee waste shall go forth from thee. Lift up thine eyes round about, and behold: all these gather themselves together, and come to thee. As I live, saith the Lord, thou shalt surely clothe thee with them all as with an ornament, and gird thyself with them, like a bride. For, as for thy waste and thy desolate places, and thy land that hath been destroyed, surely now shalt thou be too strait for the inhabitants, and they that swallowed thee up shall be far away. The children of thy bereavement shall yet say in thine ears, The place is too strait for me; give place to me that I may dwell. Then shalt thou say in thy heart, Who hath begotten me these, seeing I have been bereaved of my children, and am solitary, an exile, and wandering to and fro? and who hath brought up these? Behold, I was left alone; these, where were they?

This Scripture was given to us at the hardest time of that period of trial. I remember at times I used to wonder whether I had been deceived and deluded in being given this Scripture. Sometimes the Lord waits a long time to fulfil His Word. He kept us quite small and this word seemed never to be fulfilled. When we began to meet in the completed renovated upstairs room in 1968, almost the day we met for the first time in that room, we nearly filled it. From then on we began to expand, until literally, from that point onwards, the whole refrain in my ear was, *The place is too strait for me.* It was literally, *Thy children shall come to thee and say, It is too strait for us, give us room to dwell.*

On one occasion just before Christmas 1966 or 1967 we had the biggest Christmas love gathering we ever had. I think we had about 200 people to tea that afternoon. People were sitting with their backs to one another and there were children everywhere. I thought the overcrowding was awful. Then I felt I heard a divine chuckle. It had come to pass: *The children of thy bereavement shall yet say in thine ears, The place is too strait for me; give place to me that I may dwell.*

The ministry of those years, faithfully recorded by dear David Hilditch and Jimmy Skaife d'Ingerthorpe from approximately 1953, has since gone all over the world through tapes, CD's, transcripts, books and from the website: (www.lancelambert.org).

From those who access this website we know that the whole world is covered from mainland China to South East Asia, Australasia, India, Africa, the Middle East, South America, as well as the Western nations. We can only give the glory to God and to no one else. He has used a group of unworthy and unprofitable people, servants of His, justified alone by His grace and mercy, who learnt to listen to His voice and obey Him. It was easy at the beginning to "despise the day of small things" (see Zechariah 4:10).Everything has a beginning however small and humble it might be. If something begins with God, however small it may seem to be, it has the promise of Divine fulfilment within it. We were for the most part young people in our teens and early twenties, flung into the arms of God. He neither failed us, nor forsook us. Truly it has all been as the Lord declared: "Not by might, nor by power, but by My Spirit, saith the Lord of hosts (Zechariah 4:6b)."

6.
Love Thy Neighbour as Thyself

The Lord taught us from the beginning not only to care for one another and love one another, but to care for the unsaved person who had anything to do with us. He had said:

> When a stranger resides with you in your land, you shall
> not do him wrong. The stranger who resides with you shall
> be to you as the native among you, and you shall love
> him as yourself, for you were aliens in the land of Egypt;
> I am the Lord your God (Leviticus 19:33—34 NASB).

The apostle Paul in his letter to the Philippians had said:

> Let your [forbearing] spirit be known to all men.
> The Lord is near (Philippians 4:5 NASB).

When he said, The Lord is near, Paul meant that in the Lord Jesus was all the grace, wisdom and power which we would need to exercise a forbearing spirit and overcome.

The Messiah Jesus had summed it all up when He was asked by one of the scribes what commandment is the first of all? The Lord answered:

The first is, Hear, O Israel; The Lord our God, the Lord is one: and thou shalt love the Lord thy God with all thy heart, and with all thy soul, and with all thy mind, and with all thy strength. The second is this, Thou shalt love thy neighbour as thyself. There is none other commandment greater than these (see Mark 12:28—31).

Matthew added in his record that the Lord had also said: "On these two commandments the whole law hangeth, and the prophets." (Matthew 22:40). In other words, Jesus had said that the whole Bible is explained by the keeping of these two commandments.

Through the years that we were together we were tested on this principle. By the grace of God we overcame with love. It was not always easy. I remember one exceedingly difficult situation, which related to a brother, many thought we should tell him to leave. However, when we sought the Lord, He told us to wash the brother's feet. This we did until the Lord took him home. Our understanding of the oneness of Christ forbade us to tell any brother or sister to leave us or that they were not welcome amongst us, unless it was for heresy, persistent and unconfessed immorality, or continuous dishonest and unethical practice.

The Hullah Browns Emigrate to New Zealand

Professor Hullah Brown and his wife, who were the tenants in the residential part of the property, paid a nominal sum of £1.50 for the whole house and its sizeable garden, as we have already mentioned earlier. At the same time they let some of the rooms on the top floor of the residential house for £5 or £6 per week. There was much discussion in the fellowship about this. Someone said, "Do not make it easy for them. It is not being un-Christian. Be righteous but do not be stupid. Make it difficult for them to stay." This attitude sums up a number of comments that were made over the years.

However, when we sought the Lord in prayer, we felt that this attitude was wrong. We deemed it was our duty to love them. As we have already written, we had rebuilt their whole roof and paid for a few other works of restoration for them. To love our neighbour as we love ourselves is not always easy! Nevertheless, the Lord's words were uncompromising. We were to love the Lord our God with all our heart, and soul, and mind, and our neighbour as ourselves. In fact, with the help of the Lord our relationship with Professor Hullah Brown and Hilda became very loving. There was no rancour or bitterness in it.

Our need to possess practically the residential house was answered by the Lord in an incredible way. None of us present will ever forget it. It was in the early spring that there was a knock on the study window as always. I opened the window and there was Mrs. Hullah Brown. "I have a shock for you," she said.

She obviously could hardly contain herself. I thought, now what? Had the wall fallen down, the roof collapsed again or what?

However, she said, "Hullah (she always called him Hullah) and I are emigrating." Now he was 87 and she was 67.

I said, "What!?"

"I thought you would be surprised," she said. "We are emigrating."

"Where on earth are you going at your age?"

"To New Zealand," she said.

I exclaimed, "You cannot go farther than that."

"No," she said, "but you know our daughter is in New Zealand. We have thought a lot about it and feel it is time we went. So, we are just giving you a few months' notice, and we will be gone."

It was the happiest going in the world. First of all, they loved us when they went. In fact, they came to us and said, "We have got a house full of furniture next door and we are going to sell a lot of it. If you would like to come in and say which pieces should remain in the house, we will come to an arrangement with you." That is how many of those beautiful pieces of furniture in the residential house finally came to stay with us. Instead of making enemies we had made loving and precious friends. He blessed them and blessed us. They lived to a ripe old age and loved their last days in New Zealand.

Reconstruction of the Residential Part of the House

Once the Hullah Browns had left, much heavy work had to be done on the residential house. Floors had to come up and new beams and RSJs installed. It was discovered that the whole staircase going up three floors was resting on nothing! The beams had rotted away, so all that had to be reconstructed.

Bill Richards had also been blessed by the Lord. He was now doing building work in Rio de Janeiro and Buenos Aires. It was the Lord who brought him in suddenly to see how we were doing. As soon as he saw the work that needed to be done he offered himself. Naturally, his wages had now gone up. Nevertheless, the Lord met every expense of the reconstruction. In all, it cost £12000. All this work began in the autumn of 1975. Ivan and Blanche were living in the residential house and exercising the gift of hospitality. Whilst all the floors were torn up, Blanche had a baby son. They used the gift of hospitality which the Lord had given them to the fullest extent. It was not easy for them to live in the house whilst the work was being done. They were, however, overcomers and the Lord blessed us through them.

Miss Williamson and the Studio

When we bought Halford House in 1954, we did not realise at the time what it included. We knew that Professor Hullah Brown and Hilda were living in the residential part but had very little knowledge, if any, of their circumstances. We knew they had a controlled rent and that it was minimal. We also understood that an artist used what was called a studio in the garden. It was a simple one room shed built out of brick with a roof window that had a north facing aspect. We had no idea that the artist was not an artist and actually lived permanently in the building.

On realising this we began to investigate. To our horror we discovered an old lady in her late eighties living in the studio with a whole number of cats. I went to see her and was mortified by what I found. She had an old battered hat on her head, grime on her face, a piece of string tied around her waist and old plimsolls through which her toes were showing. In the studio in one corner was a mound of sacks on which she slept. She hardly had any furniture at all, no running water, no sanitation and no electricity. She was paying 50p a week in rent!

The most extraordinary fact about Miss Williamson was the English she spoke. It was the Queen's English, perfect County English. I realised that she must have come from a very high class family, although her appearance and lifestyle did not betray it.

I was shocked and immediately spoke with the fellowship about it. We cancelled the 50p rent per week. We ran a cable across the garden and gave her free electricity, which we found out afterwards was illegal. An army of us went in and scrubbed the place up and down, sent in fruit and flowers, brushed the cats, and did everything we could for her!

Then I remembered that Miss Williamson asked to see me. "Mr. Lambert," she said in her beautiful English, "I am very grateful for all the kindness that has been shown toward me by your church. But I would like to make it quite clear that I wish to be alone."

"Well, Miss Williamson," I replied, "if you wish to be alone, we shall respect that, but can we not do something for you?"

She said, "No, no, you cannot do anything. I wish to be alone." Then suddenly she said, "There is one thing though that troubles me! I do not get my pension."

I replied, "I will look into that for you."

"Well," she said, "that would be very kind of you."

Immediately I went and phoned up the National Health Board. They were most upset: "Sometimes this happens and these old people get overlooked; how old do you think she is?"

"Well," I said, "I understand that she is about 86 years old."

They said, " Well, then she will have a nice little nest egg coming to her, because if we find that she has not been paid her pension, she will have the whole lot which has accumulated. It will be given to her in one lump sum." They said they would look into it and get back to me.

About two or three weeks later a top man in the National Health committee phoned and said, "Mr. Lambert, we have had a special committee session this morning about your Miss Williamson."

"Oh yes, "I said, "what has happened?"

"Mr. Lambert," he replied, "we have decided that you are the one to deal with this case."

"Really," I said, "why?"

"Well," he said, "your Miss Williamson has more money than all of your people put together. We have discovered that she has a fortune in Gilt Edged Securities. Furthermore, all the interest that she is receiving from it, she refuses to touch. She is ploughing it back into the capital. Thus it is accumulating and accumulating and accumulating. For this reason she does not receive a pension! If you could persuade Miss Williamson to move she could live like a queen on the interest alone"

Then I thought to myself: how am I going to face Miss Williamson?! I went across the garden trying to look very normal and said, "Hello, Miss Williamson. Lovely day, isn't it?"

"Yes it is a nice day," she said.

"How are the cats?" I said.

She replied, "The cats are all well."

Then I said, "Miss Williamson, about your pension; it appears that you have a little money!

So she said, "How do you know that?"

"Well," I said, "it is not my business, but you did ask me to enquire about not receiving your pension. The National Health Board made the research and found out that you have this money."

Miss Williamson said, "It is not mine! I cannot touch it; it is not mine."

I said, "Then they are under a complete misapprehension; they believe it is yours! Then whose is it Miss Williamson?"

She replied, "My father's."

"Oh, Miss Williamson," I said, "is your father still alive?"

"On no," she said "he died in 1931."

"Well then," I said, "how can the money be his if he died in 1931? Did he not leave it to you?"

"Of course, he left it to me," she said.

"Well then it is yours," I said.

"No, no, no," she said. "Father was a very upright man. He was a disciplinarian. I would not dare to touch his money."

"But," I said, "Miss Williamson, if it was put into your name, it is yours. Listen: Don't touch the capital, live on the interest. If you were to live on the interest alone you could live very well. All your cats and you could move into luxury. The chairman of the National Health Committee tells me that he has been in touch with the Richmond Council, and if you would buy a property, the Council are prepared to move you and your cats into it free of charge."

Miss Williamson would not have it and she said, "No, no, never, never. Mr. Lambert, another thing is that I am not sure that once I start to use it, it would last."

Now I happened to know the sum, which was really amazing to me; it was an incredibly huge fortune, running into millions. "Miss Williamson," I said, "even if you live to be as old as Abraham, you will still have an enormous fortune to leave."

Miss Williamson died at 98 years of age in a home for the penniless, which had been years earlier a workhouse. She never touched a penny of that money and the whole lot went to the government!

There is in the story of Miss Williamson a tremendous lesson for every true believer. In our salvation God has given us everything. He is able to meet our every need according to His riches in glory in the Messiah Jesus (see Philippians 4:19). We are blessed with every spiritual blessing in the heavenly places in Christ (see Ephesians 1:3). We are made complete or full in Him (see Colossians 2:9—10). Most Christians do not experience, or live in the good of what is theirs in the Lord Jesus. They live like paupers when all the spiritual riches of God are available to them in Christ! We know in theory that all the fullness and riches and power is there in Christ, but we feel we cannot enjoy it in our experience. It is ours but we dare not touch it.

We all learnt a great lesson from the story of Miss Williamson. The Lord had enabled us to do the right thing and to care for her with love. We will never know until we are in Glory if it had any effect on her in her last hours. We learnt that we do not love to receive something in return; but as the Lord Jesus loved, not expecting a return.

The Market Garden

There was a large piece of land attached to the garden of Halford House, and it was enclosed in the original walls of the eighteenth century. It was the vegetable and fruit garden of the old manor house. The old salt stones and the barn were still at the very top of that piece of land. It was now a market garden owned by Dan Archer.

About 10 years previously, in 1957, during a time of prayer we prayed that if God was interested in that piece of ground He would give it to us. In that prayer meeting we had a great time; we did not spend much of the meeting on it, but we did "take it," in the name of the Lord, should it be His will and for His purpose. Nothing happened and years went by, and we tended to forget about it.

The Freedhold

Both sides of the property of Halford House were leasehold when we bought it. Leasehold is the temporary right to a piece of land or property. Usually, the leasehold in Great Britain was for 99 years, and then the land and property would then return to the freeholder. During these 10 years in 1960 the Grammar School Foundation, which owned the freehold of much of Richmond Hill, offered the freehold of Halford House to us for £1450. Freehold is the permanent ownership of land and the buildings on it. The money for this freehold came to us in many small amounts miraculously until we had all that we needed to purchase it.

Dan Archer's Freedhold

When we, as a fellowship of believers, were praying about the purchase of the freehold someone prayed for Dan Archer who owned the leasehold of the market garden that he would be able to purchase the freehold. A brother in the fellowship came to me afterwards and said he was prepared to give Dan Archer the money for the freehold. It was £400. Thus I went up to see Dan and offered as a fellowship of believers to pay for his freehold. He was visibly moved, but in the end bought it with his own money.

Dan Archer was a genuine Derbyshire man, a country man, and a character of the first order. He was the basis for the longest running radio series on the BBC entitled, "The Archer's." The BBC producer of those series lived on Richmond Hill and had come to know Dan Archer and was greatly impressed with him as a character and personality.

The Offer to Us of the Market Garden

Sometime in 1967 Dan Archer lumbered down the garden and came through the little wooden gate which divided our property from his. He often came down to say hello to us and have a cup of tea. Normally, he was full of fun but this time he had a face like thunder and he said to me, "Your boys have been burning my lilac bushes." "Oh," I said. "Dan, we are always telling them about those bonfires." We had two German brothers with us who loved to have bonfires, the bigger the better. I had pleaded with them to have small bonfires, but they always built larger and larger bonfires. He told them off and laughingly said, "Don't do it again." Then he sat down and had a cup of tea with us. As he got up to go he said, "Lance, I would like to have a little word with you privately." So I walked up with him and as we came to the gate he said, "I have really got to retire because I have serious kidney trouble. We are going to have to sell the market garden and move near our kids and grandchildren in Derbyshire. I told my wife Joan on the day you came and offered that money to me for the freehold, that I thought that was one of the loveliest and kindest things that anyone has ever done for me. I told Joan that the one thing I promise before God is that before I die I will give them the garden. All I want is enough money for a little cottage."

I then said, "How much would that be?"

He said, "About £12,000. I will give you a week to go down to the bank manager and talk about getting a loan."

I said, "Dan we have never done that in our lives. We will pay you in cash."

"£12,000 in cash! Well, I do not mind how it comes," Dan said. "Think about it and let me know."

He had been offered £22,000 by someone who wanted to build a multi-story car park and £25,000 by someone else who wanted to build all over it.

"You Shall Have It!"

I was so shaken that without talking to anybody else I walked back into the house and into my study and fell down on my knees and said, "Oh, Lord, please deliver me from this matter. Either it is You or it is not You. If it is of You give me peace, and if it is not please deliver me from all fear of a multi-story car park or much development." Deep in my heart I heard the voice of the Lord clearly saying, "You shall have it!" It was so ridiculous that I burst out laughing, like Sarah once did. I cannot explain it. I rose from my knees and I just had an inner conviction that God was going to fulfil this. So then I told the others.

The Prayer Meeting

That night we had our normal weekly prayer meeting. It was held in the newly completed upstairs main room, and I told them how Dan Archer had spoken to me and offered the market garden for £12,000. I thought that there would be no unanimity on this since we had a number of bills still outstanding on the upper room. Instead, there was total unanimity. Someone said, "We have to take it."

I said, "We have absolutely nothing for it."

One sister, dearly beloved by us all, said, "Well, if the Lord does not provide, we can always fall back on a mortgage."

I said, "No, no, we cannot do that; either the Lord provides or we sink." Then I said, "We must not speak to anyone outside those of us in this room; there are ears and eyes everywhere in this town. We must not speak by phone, by letter, or in careless conversation."

I phoned our solicitor, Mr. Gregg, a very precious believer, and when I told him he said, "That piece of ground is worth £100,000 at least! He is asking £12,000 you say? Goodness me, it is a gift!"

"But Mr. Gregg," I said, "we do not have the money."

"That does not matter," he said. "You have seen many miracles there, haven't you?"

So I replied, "Yes, we have."

"Well," he said, "then it is bound to happen."

The Miracle of the £12,000

Next morning I had a phone call from Lady Ogle. She said, "Lance, would you come and talk with me about that market garden?"

I said to her, "Oh, no, I cannot! Who told you? No one is supposed to have said anything. I could not possibly come, for it would damage the Lord's Name. Everyone last night swore together not to tell anyone."

"Just wait; come off your high horse," she replied. "Just give me the chance to say something! The Lord woke me up at 5 o'clock this morning and said, 'Don't buy the house, buy the garden.' I have been phoning my friends all over the place to see if anyone knows of a garden for sale. Nobody knew of such a sale, except Elizabeth Stearns (the daughter of T. Austin-Sparks)."

Elizabeth had said, "Oh, Lance has told you about the market garden, has he?"

Lady Ogle said, "No, he has not."

Elizabeth then said, "Then you had better get in touch with Lance immediately!"

Lady Ogle said to me, "How much is this garden?"

I told her, and she then said: "The Lord has spoken to me about this matter. I will arrange for you to have this £12,000 in cash within 24 hours."

To complete the miracle I received an excited call from Mr. Gregg who said: "Lady Ogle's solicitor has an office opposite mine across the street and is coming with £12,000 in cash for the market garden. He only has to walk across the road." The sale of the market garden was completed within a few days.

Love Thy Neighbour as Thyself

It was our love and concern for Dan Archer that sparked the thought in his heart to give the first offer of the market garden to us. He himself said to Joan his wife, "It was one of the loveliest and kindest things ever done to me." So strong was his feeling that he would not take much larger offers.

When Professor Hullah Brown and Hilda his wife emigrated to New Zealand, they went without any bitter feelings or rancour, but instead with love in their hearts for us. We had learnt to love and serve Miss Williamson as much as she would allow without any thought of a return from her. With this love of God in our hearts, in spite of being very ordinary and often failing believers, the way for the Lord to act was opened.

7.
The Five Basic and Essential Lessons-Part I

The restoration and renovation of Halford House were miraculous. As a fellowship we had experienced miracle after miracle of His leading and provision. Yet it is a remarkable fact that we were a company of believers who did not believe that the church was a physical building or a mere human organisation. We believed that the house of the Lord was made up of living stones; those who were redeemed and born of God. Never at any time did we believe that Halford House was the house of the Lord. It was the believers meeting there, who were the Lord's house.

The Significance of the Restoration of Halford House

Why was the Lord leading us in this manner? Some of the miracles were phenomenal. In fact, from all that the Lord did it would seem that He was interested in the physical and the material. At one point we had so much furniture that we could hardly move.

We began to give some of it away and to simplify the rooms. The Lord answered, however, by providing more and more. It dawned on me that He was trying to say something to us, and we began to seek Him for clarity.

There had been a certain amount of criticism both within the fellowship and from the other churches in the area. We had countered that, as I have already mentioned, by trying to simplify the rooms. I remembered how brother T. Austin-Sparks had quoted from a letter to him by Watchman Nee. Brother Nee had written: "You know, I have learned from the Lord to face every criticism by asking the Lord, is it true? Can I learn anything from it? In this way I have taken the sting out of the scorpion's tail!" Maybe the motive behind the criticism that came to us was wrong or even evil, but was there something we could learn from it? Nevertheless, however much we sought to have a right attitude to the criticism and tried to placate the critics, the Lord sent us yet more items of furniture.

Was the Lord meaning by all these miracles which He did that He wanted to give every company of God's children an old house, nationally graded as an ancient monument? Or that He would miraculously provide for the restoration and renovation of such, even providing all the furniture and furnishings in keeping with the period of the house? Was the Lord interested in antiques or had He great interest in period furniture?

The Lord is not interested in mere perishable bricks and mortar; why then did He do all this with us? What could it possibly mean? After all, what He did with us was extraordinary! Why did He do it?

Halford House a Divine Sign

As a result of all these questions, I began to seek the Lord seriously. I asked the Lord to explain to me why He had done all this. Suddenly, in my spirit I heard a clear voice: "The day of signs is not over." Then I said to Him: "Lord, do you mean this house is a sign?" The Lord said, "It is a sign, and you shall never again take anything I have given to it and give it away or sell it." So I rested in the Lord from that day forward. Every miracle which the Lord had performed could either be a venue of revelation and illumination or a stumbling block. Everywhere you find a Divine sign recorded in the Word of God, one realises that it either leads to salvation or to loss and judgment; either into a new discovery and experience of the Lord Himself or something over which we trip. For example, the healings which the Lord Jesus performed either brought people to Him or made them vehemently antagonistic. In this manner Divine signs divide.

If Halford House is a Divine sign, the miracles of its restoration and renovation make sense. When we first came together, our burden was for awakening and revival. We felt there was so much that was wrong with twentieth century Christianity. It lacked the organic nature of the early church, the sense of belonging to the Lord Jesus as supreme Head, and to one another as members of His body. In all the initiatives throughout church history, which the Lord Jesus has launched by the Holy Spirit, these qualities have reappeared again and again.

The Five Basic and Essential Lessons

From the story of the recovery, restoration and renovation of Halford House we learnt five basic and essential lessons. What the Lord did amongst us in the rebuilding of the house was a picture book, signifying vital and essential truths in the restoration and rebuilding of the House of the Lord.

God Desires a Dwelling Place

The first basic lesson was that God desires a habitation or a *home*. In the beginning we were not clear as to the nature of the church. Gradually, the Lord revealed to us its spiritual nature and meaning. He used Halford House, its recovery and restoration, as a picture book of what He longs for and desires in His people.

It is summed up in the simple words of the Lord in Psalm 132: 13–16:

> *For the Lord hath chosen Zion; He hath desired it for his habitation. This is my resting-place for ever: Here will I dwell; for I have desired it. I will abundantly bless her provision: I will satisfy her poor with bread. Her priests also will I clothe with salvation; and her saints shall shout aloud for joy.*

The Heart Attitude Required in Us

To reach this end requires the same spirit and determination that was found in King David:

Surely I will not come into the tabernacle of my house, nor
go up into my bed; I will not give sleep to mine eyes, or
slumber to mine eyelids; until I find out a place for the Lord,
a tabernacle for the Mighty One of Jacob (Psalm 132:3—5).

Or again:

One thing have I asked of the Lord, that will I seek
after: that I may dwell in the house of the Lord all
the days of my life, to behold the beauty of the Lord,
and to enquire in his temple (Psalm 27:4).

No wonder the Lord said of David: "He was a man after His own heart"! All of this came as a thunderous revelation from the Lord to the hearts of us young people. We had been flung into the arms of God, and our one desire and purpose was that the House of the Lord should be built.

The Desire of the Lord for a Home

The Hebrew for the English word *habitation* is *Moshav*, "a dwelling place or dwelling." In Israel today a Moshav is a community or a co-operative where people live together and share everything. This matter of God seeking a habitation is one of the major themes of the Bible. If one takes a concordance and looks up the references under these headings, one discovers how much of the Bible is encompassed—the House of the Lord, the Temple, the Tabernacle, Dwelling Place, Habitation, Resting Place, Zion.

We had been led of God to purchase and possess a house. The Lord then turned that house into a habitation, a home. From this we learnt that the desire and purpose of God from the beginning was to have a dwelling place amongst men. The first time it was mentioned in the Bible was when God appeared to Jacob and gave him a vision in a dream of His Eternal Purpose. Jacob called it the House of God and the gate of Heaven; in Hebrew, *Beit El* (see Genesis 28:17). The Tabernacle of God and the Temple of God occupy a vital place in the Bible. Indeed, the life of God's people was essentially centred symbolically in either the Tabernacle or the Temple.

In the New Testament it is explained in the words of the apostle Paul to the church in Ephesus:

> *In whom each several building, fitly framed together, groweth into a holy temple in the Lord; in whom ye also are builded together for a habitation of God in the Spirit (Ephesians 2:21—22).*

And again the apostle Peter writes:

> *Unto whom coming, a living stone... ye also, as living stones, are built up a spiritual house, to be a holy priesthood, to offer up spiritual sacrifices, acceptable to God through Jesus Christ (I Peter 2:4—5).*

When we come to the end of the Bible it is summed up in the words of the apostle John:

And I heard a great voice out of the throne saying, Behold,
the tabernacle of God is with men, and he shall dwell
with them, and they shall be his peoples, and God himself
shall be with them, and be their God (Revelation 21:3).

Then again: And I saw no temple therein: for the Lord God the Almighty, and the Lamb, are the temple thereof (Revelation 21:22.) From this we discover that the Lord God and the Lamb are God's Temple and House.

The Almighty God desired from the beginning to dwell amongst us. In Sunday school language He describes His longing to find His home in us. He called it: "my resting place forever: here will I dwell; for I have desired it." It is staggering to realise that the Almighty longs for such a relationship and fellowship with the human beings whom He has redeemed. This intimacy and proximity we see in the figures employed by the Holy Spirit in the Bible—the oneness of the Head and the body; the Bridegroom and the bride; the husband and the wife.

This House of the Lord, this Temple which He is building, is not a physical and material structure, inanimate and lifeless, a human organisation set up by man; it is made up of those whom He redeems and saves in a living organic union with Himself. It is a union with God in Christ and a communion of all those whom He saves and who are in Him. That is His eternal home.

It is not enough academically to know the truth and the doctrine, but it requires a total commitment on the part of those whom the Lord saves. We have to have the same spirit that David had when he said: "One thing have I asked of the Lord, that will I seek after: That I may dwell in the house of the Lord all the days of my life (Psalm 27:4a)." It was a consuming passion that would not let him rest until it was fulfilled. And so it must be with us!

Other Foundation Can No Man Lay

The second basic and essential lesson is to do with foundations. When we bought Halford House there was a lot that had to be done with the foundation. We had been told that the house had no foundation, but we discovered later that there was an old but somewhat inadequate eighteenth-century foundation. It had been covered up in the war years during the blackout, incredibly, for fear that light would be seen through it! The foundation had to be strengthened and in one case a whole wall had to be completely rebuilt on a new foundation.

The Foundation of the Church is the Lord Jesus Alone

The Word of God has much to say about foundations; after all a house or building takes its shape from its foundation. It is all important. The Lord Jesus had said: "Upon this rock I will build My church (Matthew 16:18b)." That rock is Himself. It is His Being and Character, His Word, His Finished Work, His Resurrection Life and Power, and His present position at the right hand of the Father in heaven. Upon that solid rock alone the Lord Jesus builds His church. As the apostle Paul, by the Holy Spirit, writes: "For other foundation can no man lay than that which is laid, which is Jesus Christ." (1 Corinthians 3:11).

If the foundation upon which we build the church is a false foundation, the whole building will crumble. The Word of God, which our Lord Jesus personifies, cannot be altered, brought up to date, made more acceptable to contemporary society, or made to suit our own opinions and outlook. Such tampering with the foundation, once and for all laid, can only bring spiritual powerlessness, lifelessness, and apostasy. It is the dry rot and wood boring beetle of which we saw so much in Halford House. This kind of problem is never seen at the beginning. It manifests itself only as time passes and results in total breakdown.

We "green" young people saw clearly that the only foundation upon which we could meet was Christ alone. We began to see the supremacy and all sufficiency of the Lord Jesus. He was to us the Beginning and the End, the First and the Last; He was to be everything in the church.

Everything Built on the Foundation Must Be of Christ

The Lord said:

> *Behold, I lay in Zion for a foundation a stone, a tried stone,*
> *a precious corner-stone of sure foundation (Isaiah 28:16a).*

That foundation stone is the Messiah, the Lord Jesus. As we have already stated, there is no other church foundation. Isaiah also prophesied: "The Lord of hosts, him shall ye sanctify; ... and He shall be for a sanctuary." (Isaiah 8:13a—14a). It is entirely noteworthy that the Lord **Himself** is called a *sanctuary*. The word in Hebrew is, *Miqdash*, which means "the Tabernacle or Temple and its precincts." In the Word of God the Lord Jesus is described as the Chief Cornerstone of the foundation from which the whole building takes its line (see Mark 12:10;

Ephesians 2:20). He is the Top Stone, the completion of the whole building (see Zechariah 4:7).

In other words, it is the Lord Jesus through whom and out of whom everything is built on that foundation. Humanism, human philosophy, the wisdom of this world has no place in it; neither has psychological manipulation! As the apostle Paul writes concerning the church: Christ is all and in all. He is everything in everyone (see Colossians 3:11; Ephesians 1:23). He is All to the church.

The Centrality and Sufficiency of the Lord Jesus

Foundational to the church—its beginnings, its sources, the process of its building and its completion—is the centrality and sufficiency of the Lord Jesus. He is the Beginning and the End, and all the development that is in between. Christ is the Beginning and the End of our salvation. There is no salvation whatsoever outside of Him. In that salvation is all the sufficiency that we could possibly need. Christ is also the Beginning and the End and the growth to fullness and maturity in our Christian life. It is all in His resurrection life and power. Christ is also the Beginning and the End of church life; the process of being built together and built up in Him; the functioning of the priesthood of all believers. Christ is the Beginning and the End of our service, or should be! If we are contributing gold, silver and precious stone it is Himself that we are contributing; if it is wood, hay and stubble, it is our flesh that we are contributing (see 1 Corinthians 3:11–14)!

The Practical Unity of All Believers

The unity of all believers is found alone on this foundation of Christ. If the Lord has received a person, can we reject him or her? Our fellowship has to be with all whom the Lord has saved without distinction of colour, race, nationality, or gender. In the Lord Jesus we are all one new man. The middle wall of partition has been destroyed and we have been made one. Therefore, we should be careful of anything which places some believers inside and others outside. It was as a result of this truth dawning on us that we refused to have a church membership which would divide some believers from other believers.

Apart from heresy, acts of immorality and dishonest unethical practice, we have no right to excommunicate or make unwelcome anyone who is born of God.

The only division allowed by the Word of God between believers is not denominational but geographic. As far as the Lord is concerned we who are born of God are one people universally. It is a question of where we live.

The apostle Peter, having spoken of us as living stones being built up a spiritual house to be a holy priesthood and to offer up spiritual sacrifices acceptable to God, continues and writes:

> But you are a chosen race, a royal priesthood, a holy
> nation, a people for God's own possession, that you may
> proclaim the excellencies of Him who has called you out
> of darkness into His marvellous light (1 Peter 2:9 NASB).

He makes no distinction between those who are born of God. We are one chosen race, one royal priesthood, and one holy nation.

We are to be those living stones built up together **in the place where we are living**, acting as a holy priesthood, offering up spiritual sacrifices to God, acceptable through Jesus the Messiah. In the fellowship of believers meeting at Halford House, this was the understanding we had almost from the beginning. It became more and more clear.

Christ as Our Covering

The third basic and essential lesson is to know Christ as our Covering. This is a strategically vital matter, and especially so for the days in which we are now living. As soon as we bought Halford House we had to deal with the main roof of the meeting side of the property. The roof had leaked for years allowing both snow and water into the house. As a result there was much dry rot and wood boring beetles. These two problems work silently. You never hear them and only know the destruction they have caused when you fall through the floor. It is the same with church life. If we do not heed the necessity of covering, spiritual dry rot and spiritual boring beetles do their silent and destructive work. Far from the building work of the church progressing, it is being undermined and destroyed.

Amongst believers there is much ignorance of this essential matter. As a result there are many casualties. The Lord has not saved us to throw us out uncovered, unarmed, and unprepared for the battle in which we find ourselves. He has made full provision for our safety and security. Indeed, His goal is that we should not be 'survivors' but overcomers! This is why Satan intensely focuses on this matter; it is his one aim and strategy. Satan uses the ignorance of the believer, the unawareness we have of the covering the Lord has provided, and the manner in which He has equipped us for the conflict.

What is Spiritual Covering?

To understand how essential this matter is, we need to realise that the word translated in English, to atone or atonement, used throughout the Old Testament is in Hebrew, Kaphar—"to cover" or "to be covered." There was no way to approach God or anything to do with Him, except through atonement. It was a perfect picture of the coming Lamb of God, through whose blood we would be covered and reconciled to God. We see this even more clearly in the words of the apostle John when he writes:

> *Now is come the salvation, and the power, and the kingdom*
> *of our God, and the authority of his Christ: for the accuser*
> *of our brethren is cast down, who accuseth them before*
> *our God day and night. And they overcame him because*
> *of the blood of the Lamb (Revelation 12:10—11a).*

Through the finished and complete work of the Lord Jesus, these believers, covered by the blood of the Lamb, overcame. As the apostle Paul said:

> *For He delivered us from the domain of darkness,*
> *and transferred us to the kingdom of His beloved*
> *Son, in whom we have redemption, the forgiveness*
> *of sin (Colossians 1:13—14 NASB).*

The Safety and Security of the Believer

In the Old Testament, in particular, we have a whole number of figures which are used to convey this idea of covering. They all speak of the safety and security of the people of God. For example: Stronghold; Fortress; Refuge; High Tower; Strong Tower; High Place; Shelter; and Shield. These terms are much used in the Old Testament. For example:

*The Lord is the **stronghold** of my life (Psalm 27:1b mg).*

*The Lord is their strength, and he is a **stronghold** of salvation to his anointed (Psalm 28:8).*

*The name of the Lord is a **strong tower;** the righteous runneth into it, and is safe (Proverbs 18:10).*

*The Lord is my rock, and my **fortress,** and my deliverer; my God, my rock, in whom I will take **refuge;** my **shield,** and the horn of my salvation, my **high tower** (Psalm 18:2).*

The people of God need continuously to experience Christ as their shelter and defence. These are all pictures of being **in Him.**

In Christ

There is no greater safety or security to be found anywhere than to be "in Christ." These two words unlock the New Testament. If we would learn how to remain where God has placed us when we first believed, we would be immovable and invincible. Can Satan remove Christ or conquer Christ? The answer is simply:

It is impossible! The weakest believer who is in Christ is absolutely safe and secure. It is for this reason that Satan has to lure us out of the one place in which we are absolutely safe. When we first believed, God the Father by the Holy Spirit positioned us in Christ! In Him He gave us everything—the faith, the grace, the power, the wisdom and so much else.

Is it any wonder that the Holy Spirit through the apostle Paul writes:

Finally, be strong in the Lord, and in the strength of his might. Put on the whole armor of God, that ye may be able to stand against the wiles of the devil. For our wrestling is not against flesh and blood, but against the principalities, against the powers, against the world-rulers of this darkness, against the spiritual hosts of wickedness in the heavenly places. Wherefore take up the whole armor of God, that ye may be able to withstand in the evil day, and, having done all, to stand (Ephesians 6:10—13).

In the Roman letter Paul, by the Spirit, writes: "But put ye on the Lord Jesus Christ, and make not provision for the flesh." (Romans 13:14a). The armour of God or the armour of light is the Lord Jesus Himself. In Him we are properly equipped and clothed for the battle.

Abide in Me and I in You

The Lord Jesus summed up this matter of covering in the last major statement He made before His arrest and death:

I am the true vine, and my Father is the husbandman ...
Abide in me, and I in you. As the branch cannot bear fruit
of itself, except it abide in the vine; so neither can ye, except
ye abide in me. I am the vine, ye are the branches: He that
abideth in me, and I in him, the same beareth much fruit:
for apart from me ye can do nothing (John 15:1, 4—5).

Of all the remarkable truths which the Lord uttered to the apostles, this must have been one of the most extraordinary. The vine had always been a symbol of the covenant people of God, those who were the redeemed of the Lord. How could Jesus say, "I am the covenant people of God, and My Father is the husbandman." He then explained Himself, saying: "Abide in me, and I in you." Dwell or remain in Me and I in you, and then said, "For apart from me ye can do nothing." If we do not remain where God has positioned us, where He has placed us in His grace and mercy, not only are we barren, but we can do nothing! What a commentary on so much Christian life, service and work.

The essential message in what the Lord Jesus was saying is simple; remain where God has positioned you—**In Christ**. He will then remain **in us** to be everything we need. He will also be the life, the work, and the testimony of the church, as well as the family and the life of the individual believer.

From all of this we understand how vital this subject of covering is. It spells the difference between growth and stuntedness, between victory and defeat, between fruitfulness and barrenness. It is as essential for the individual believer as for the church.

Exterior of residential part, seen from Halford Road

Entrance to meeting rooms; porch under construction

Eric Luck wiring doorbell push

The entrance completed

Old staircase, later rebuilt to the left

Bill Richards at work in meeting room

Meeting room before start of work

Meeting room cleared for work to begin

*Bill Richards' sign (with old 'Gents',
the low building to the left)*

RSJs to support meeting room roof

Meeting room ceiling rafters

New wall with provision for bay windows to meeting room

Newly blocked windows between meeting room and library

Bay windows and panelling work in meeting room

Meeting room, fire escape door and baptistry;
also new wall panels

Meeting room ready for use

Library restoration

Library restored, before bookshelves built

8.
The Five Basic and Essential Lessons- Part II

The Word of God Which Liveth and Abideth

When we bought Halford House, there was no electricity in the meeting side of the property. Therefore one of the first basic and essential necessities was to install electrical power. With this we come to the fourth basic and essential lesson. It is the absolute necessity of light; without light we wander in darkness. We do not see clearly, but only see dim outlines, even if those. The result is confusion.

The Word of God is the light that we need. The psalmist declares: "Thy word is a lamp unto my feet, and light unto my path." (Psalm 119:105). And again he writes: "The opening of thy words giveth light; it giveth understanding unto the simple (Psalm 119:130)." And yet again: "For with thee is the fountain of life: in thy light shall we see light." (Psalm 36:9). We have here firstly the written Word of God as the light which is given to us; and secondly, the necessity of the Holy Spirit's work in giving us illumination. Truly it is: In thy light shall we see light.

The Living and Active Word of God

The apostle Paul wrote these words to Timothy:

> *All Scripture is inspired by God and profitable for teaching,*
> *for reproof, for correction, for training in righteousness;*
> *so that the man of God may be adequate, equipped*
> *for every good work (II Timothy 3:16—17 NASB).*

It is noteworthy that the Word of God is not merely a written or printed word, but is alive. Through the Holy Spirit it is able to mould, form and equip the man or woman of God, for every good work. To express this in a different way, the Bible is not inanimate words, but from the day it was given and written it was alive and active. So alive that the apostle Peter writes:

> *Having been **begotten again**, not of corruptible seed,*
> *but of incorruptible, **through the word of God,** which*
> *liveth and abideth. For, all flesh is as grass, and all the*
> *glory thereof as the flower of grass. The grass withereth,*
> *and the flower falleth: but the word of the Lord abideth*
> *for ever (I Peter 1:23—25a; author's emphasis).*

Through His Word we are born again!

With this the writer of the Hebrew letter by the Holy Spirit totally agrees:

*For the word of God is **living,** and **active,** and sharper than*
any two-edged sword, and piercing even to the dividing
of soul and spirit (Hebrews 4:12a; author's emphasis).

This is not a mere printed word; it is alive and creative. The Greek word *energos,* translated in the ASV as *active,* means "creative" or "operative" or "working." We find this truth everywhere we look in the Bible. For example we are to "receive with meekness the **implanted** word (see James 1:21 author's emphasis)." Indeed, the Lord Jesus speaks of the Word as being good seed which takes root and grows up and bears much fruit (see Matthew 13:23). The apostle Paul commands us with these words: "Let the word of Christ **dwell** in you richly (Colossians 3:16a; author's emphasis)." The Word of God has within it the living and operative power to realise the purpose of God. It was never meant merely to satisfy human intellect, but rather to carry into effect the will and purpose of God in those born of God.

The apostle John declares: "God is light, and in him is no darkness at all (1 John 1:5b)." Through the written Word, God speaks to us; and it is the Holy Spirit who illuminates that Word to us and then makes it real in us. The Lord Jesus is the personification, the full expression in flesh and in practice, of the written Word of God.

A Spirit of Wisdom and Revelation
in the Knowledge of Christ

From all that we have written, we see that the Word of God in its every part is essential to our spiritual well-being and growth to maturity. Without a living experience of God speaking to us through His Word, all we have is "religion." We can have the routine, the ritual, the organisation, and the methodology, but the Lord Himself has long departed from it. Without the Holy Spirit using the Word of God to bring revelation to us concerning the character of God and His Eternal Purpose, and at the same time realising the indwelling of Christ in us, we have nothing but religiosity.

From all of this, it should be clear that there is no alternative to the living Word of God and the work of the Holy Spirit in illuminating it. It is no wonder that when the apostle Paul was writing the letter to the church in Ephesus, he stopped for a moment to explain to that church the prayer burden in his heart. He wrote:

> *For this cause I also, having heard of the faith in the Lord*
> *Jesus which is among you, and the love which ye show toward*
> *all the saints, cease not to give thanks for you, making*
> *mention of you in my prayers; that the God of our Lord*
> *Jesus Christ, the Father of glory, may give unto you a spirit*
> *of wisdom and revelation in the knowledge of him; having*
> *the eyes of your heart enlightened, that ye may know what*
> *is the hope of his calling, what the riches of the glory of his*
> *inheritance in the saints, and what the exceeding greatness*
> *of his power to us-ward who believe (Ephesians 1:15—19a).*

Paul was so afraid that his letter would be merely words. The church in Ephesus needed to have a spirit of wisdom and revelation in their knowledge of the Lord Jesus if they were to understand the letter and experience all that was theirs in Him.

The Authority, Inspiration and Relevance of God's Word

The authority, the inspiration, and the relevance of God's Word are essential to the health of the church and the work of the Gospel. Anything that invalidates or devalues His Word is to be shunned and avoided. The attempts to bring God's Word up to date, to make it more contemporary and relevant to modern society, reveals an evil heart of unbelief. God's Word is utterly relevant to every age. The concept that there are parts of the Word of God which are obsolete, and therefore to be ignored, leads only to backsliding and apostasy. It means that the church in seeking to be contemporary and relevant, in fact becomes dated and irrelevant. It then becomes confusion and has no testimony to the age in which it lives.

When the House of God is truly the **House of God**, it has enormous impact upon the society in which it is found. It is like a light shining in the darkness, like a city set on a hill. In the Word of God, we are called to be:

Blameless and harmless, children of God without blemish in the midst of a crooked and perverse generation, among whom ye are seen as lights in the world, holding forth the word of life (Philippians 2:15—16).

This has been illustrated in the many great initiatives which the Lord Jesus has launched in church history. These have transformed whole nations, and impacted their society. When men and women are delivered and saved, born of the Spirit of God and transformed, it is a consequence and product of the holding forth of the Word of life. It is an illustration that the Word of the Lord is living and creatively powerful. His Word needs no defending. Its power, when preached to bring men and women into a living union with God in Christ, is its own defence.

The Water of Life

When we bought Halford House, there was no adequate water supply in the meeting side of the property. It was one of the first essentials to be corrected. We thus come to the fifth basic lesson. In the Word of God water is always an illustration of life. Without water life dies.

Through the resurrection of the Lord Jesus the church became a possibility. On Calvary He finished the work of our salvation; henceforward any hopeless sinner who drew near to God through the Lord Jesus would be saved. It was, however, the resurrection of the Messiah which opened the possibility of the church being born. Nonetheless, it was the pouring out of the Holy Spirit, the Spirit of Life, on the day of Pentecost that brought the church to that birth. Then the possibility became a factual reality!

On that day, for the first time ever in world history, one hundred and twenty human beings saved by the grace of God were joined in a living union to the Lord Jesus at the right hand of God. That union, whilst lived in and experienced, was to turn the whole known world upside down. Without all the paraphernalia of modern missions, within hours 3000 people were saved and entered the same union with God in the Messiah. Within weeks they had reached 5000, and within months thousands more. This incredible work of the Holy Spirit was to turn not only the Jewish world upside down but also the Roman world.

Whilst in a living union with their Head and Saviour, the church was unstoppable and unbeatable. Even though they died in the thousands as martyrs, it could not stop the triumph of their crucified Messiah. The secret was the resurrection life and power of the Lord Jesus. He was their risen and enthroned Messiah.

Everything about the church in those early days was the practical expression of this resurrection life and power. It was like a great river of living water bringing life to a desert. Everywhere it came, life and fruit were the result.

The Church Alive and Growing Through Christ's Life

Describing the church the apostle Peter wrote:

> *Unto whom coming, a **living** stone, rejected indeed of men, but with God elect, precious, ye also, as **living** stones, are built up a spiritual house (1 Peter 2:4—5a; (author's emphasis).*

When also describing the church, the apostle Paul writes:

> *In whom each several building, fitly framed together, **groweth** into a holy temple in the Lord (Ephesians 2:21; author's emphasis).*

Or again:

> *But speaking truth in love, may **grow up** in all things into him, who is the head, even Christ; from whom all the body fitly framed and knit together through that which every joint*

supplieth, *according to the working in due measure of each several part,* **maketh the increase** *of the body unto the building up of itself in love (Ephesians 4:15—16; author's emphasis).*

The terms used in these Scriptures do not convey something static or inanimate, but rather alive and growing. These are but a very few of many Scriptures which reveal that the church is a living, growing entity.

The Church— the Head and Body

In my estimation, the clearest way in which we see the church as a living and growing organism is in the term "Head and body." This is a term exclusively used in the New Testament. Very often, the Lord Jesus as the Head of the church is seen as a president or a prime minister of a nation or the chancellor of a university or a principal of a school or a hospital. Likewise, "the body" is seen as a corporation or a community apart from the Head. The term, which the Holy Spirit introduces in the New Testament, is however revolutionary. Nothing like this was ever mentioned in the Old Testament. If you sever a head from its body you have neither a living head nor a living body. The head belongs to the body and the body belongs to the head; it is one living organism.

The Secret of the Church's Invincibility

This was the secret of the church in the New Testament. Just as the intelligence and the will is in the head and is then communicated to the body, so it was with the early church. It was the ability to hear and understand the Head, which gave that church its extraordinary power and impact. It is, of course, the work of the Holy Spirit to make the will and mind of the Head known to the body. Whilst the church dwelt in obedience to its Head, it was invincible.

Through That Which Every Joint Supplies

It was the measure in which each member of the body of the Lord Jesus was experiencing His resurrection life and power that determined the growth of the church and its health. As soon as the church began to rely on its routine, its organisation, and methodology, it became lifeless! This was the problem in making a huge difference between the "clergy and the laity." This will always result in a large number of people led and spoon-fed who never grow up into maturity. It is also the problem when there is a "pastor complex." The pastor does everything—he hears the Lord, he leads the flock, he contributes the Word—and the body is then made up of spectators. The fact is simple: if the members of the body do not contribute the life of the Lord Jesus, they do not grow. They waste away. It is therefore essential that we give as well as receive. It is a law of the health of the body.

The Priesthood of All Believers

This tremendous and vital truth, the priesthood of all believers, was mainly rediscovered in the Reformation and has remained part of the doctrine of all the Protestant denominations. Although that is true, in practice it was lost by the growing emphasis on the difference between the clergy and the laity. Gradually, the practice of the priesthood of all believers ceased. In some groups which preceded the Reformation it had been practised. During the Reformation and after it, the Anabaptists, the Mennonites, and other such groups practised it; as also did the Quakers, the Brethren and the Pentecostals.

The fact is that when the priesthood of all believers is not practised, it results in a lack of spiritual growth in believers. The spiritual law that governs growth to maturity is to contribute what you have of the Lord, so that you may receive more of the Lord. We have in Israel an incredible illustration of this in the Dead Sea which is the lowest place in the whole earth!! Nothing lives in the Dead Sea—neither fish, nor crab, nor crayfish— nor any other living thing. The Lake of Galilee is totally different; it abounds in every kind of life. Why is there such a difference between these two lakes? The difference is simple. The Lake of Galilee receives all the water from the Golan and Mount Hermon, and gives it in an outflow through the Jordan valley or through the National Water Carrier, which conveys it to the rest of Israel. The Dead Sea receives everything and gives nothing! It even takes the life giving water of the Lake of Galilee and makes it sterile. When believers receive everything and contribute nothing they become as sterile and fruitless as the Dead Sea.

Let All Things Be Done Unto Building Up

These five basic and essential principles must operate if the House of the Lord is to be built. There is no way in which even one of them can be overlooked. They are all essential to the building up of the body of Christ. Even a superficial reading of much of the New Testament would bring us to the conclusion that the matter of "building," of "being built up," is vital. The apostle Paul writes to the church at Corinth: "So also ye, since ye are zealous of spiritual gifts, seek that ye may abound unto the edifying (the building up) of the church." (1 Corinthians 14:12). And also: "Let all things be done unto edifying (building up) 14:26b." (author's note). To the church in Rome he writes: "So then let us pursue the things which make for peace and the building up of one another." (Romans 14:19 NASB). The Greek word *Oikodome*, translated by the English word "edify" means "building up."

Spiritual Dry Rot and Wood Boring Beetles

If there is anything faulty in the foundation or in the roofing, dry rot and wood boring beetles can manifest themselves. Certainly this was true of Halford House. The fact was that much damp arose from a faulty foundation and from roofing that was not water tight. Satan and his host are always watching for an opportunity. The Lord Jesus said: "The thief cometh not, but that he may steal, and kill, and destroy: I came that they may have life, and may have it abundantly (John 10:10)." Dry rot and wood boring beetles are exactly like this; they steal, kill and destroy. So often it is not apparent, and only in its last stages does it make itself known. When we experience the life of the Lord Jesus in fullness, it keeps the individual believer and the church free from spiritual dry rot and the action of spiritual wood boring beetles!

Both the abundant resurrection life and the power of the Lord Jesus act as a protection from these problems. It is a fact that even when the foundations were originally good, over the years spiritual dry rot and wood boring beetles can destroy so much. It wrecks what was once a living home of God and renders it unliveable. It then becomes only the House of God in name.

Indeed, it can become a nest of demons. A good example is the church at Laodicea. The Lord Jesus, the Head and Saviour of the church, was outside of it and knocking on its door (see Revelation 3:14—22). None of the elders or deacons or the other responsible leaders recognised this reality. That company of believers had an incredible corporate self-estimate! The Lord's estimate of them was totally different.

The Bible, which they honoured, studied and believed, by that point in time must have been academically approached by them. Certainly it was not experienced as: "The word of God is living, and active, and sharper than any two-edged sword, and piercing even to the dividing of soul and spirit." (Hebrews 4:12). Otherwise, the Holy Spirit, by the Word of God, could have revealed their condition. Incredibly, this company of believers rumbled on without any idea of their true state, impervious to the voice of the Lord and Saviour.

It is a necessity that every child of God, every member of the body of our Lord Jesus, has his or her own original and daily experience of the resurrection life and power of the Messiah. No amount of mental head knowledge of the Bible can be a substitute for daily walking with the Lord. It is the experience of Him that will keep any child of God from spiritual dry rot and spiritual wood boring beetles!

9.
The Church–the Dwelling Place and Home of God

There were other lessons we learnt from the restoration and renovation of Halford House. The Lord did not leave the house in a clean clinical state; He turned it into a home. This is vastly different from a house beautifully restored and renovated, but still only a structure. The foundations could be there, the covering roofs in order, the basic amenities of light and water installed, and still it could resemble a medical or dental clinic. It could be clean and restored, but sterile!

A House Turned into a Home

The Lord turned a restored and renovated building into a home. The manner in which He did it was miraculous. Piece after piece of furniture came, much of it in keeping with the old manor house. When it was put together it turned the house from being a mere institution into a home.

From this we learnt a tremendous lesson. The House of God is to be the dwelling place, "the home" of God. The church is not a mere institution, although our Lord Jesus did institute it when He said: "Upon this rock I will build my church." (Matthew 16:18). An institution can be cold, clinical and lifeless, but the church is to be warm, living, and full of the Presence of the Lord. It is meant to be the expression of the love and grace of the Lord Jesus. Likewise, the church is not a mere human organisation. It has organisation but it is of a different order. It is like the human body which has an incredible organisation, all developing from its organic life. The Holy Spirit causes the church to develop in such a manner that the different callings and offices are filled by the right people. It is obvious that these callings and offices have to be recognised by an assembly of believers. It is, however, recognition of what the Lord has produced; the character, the gift and the spiritual growth can be seen by all in those who are to be leaders and who are to fill the offices. Neither is the church a "Divine civil service," coldly efficient, dutifully responsible, and doctrinally correct! There, everything it preaches is correct but there is no heart. So often that is the only level to which a church rises.

One could rightly say that from the beginning God has desired to be at home amongst human beings. He wants to express Himself to the world through the warmth of a spiritual home. He does not want to be some remote, unapproachable and impersonal God. We catch a glimpse of this in the manner in which the Lord daily sought fellowship with Adam and Eve in the Garden of Eden (see Genesis 3:8—10). It was the home and family which God was seeking if only they had taken of the Tree of Life.

It is a fact that fallen and sinful mankind is homeless. Within every human being is a desire for a spiritual home. This desire, generally undefined and unrecognised, is a longing implanted by God within unsaved human beings. The Word of God describes this longing when it declares: He hath set eternity in their heart (Ecclesiastes 3:11b). The church, as the Home of God, was from its inception at Pentecost to be the answer to that yearning. When God is "at home" and meets homeless sinners, men and women are saved. The apostle Paul alludes to this when he writes that an unsaved man will: "fall down on his face and worship God, declaring that God is among you indeed." (1 Corinthians 14:25b). It is the missing feature in so many congregations of God's people.

God "at Home" in the Lord Jesus

We see what the church is meant to be when we look at the Lord Jesus. From the beginning God had this desire for a dwelling place, a resting place, a home in which, and by which, He could express and reveal Himself. In the first words of the Bible we read that the Holy Spirit, who has always been the supervisor and manager of God's purpose and work, was: "brooding upon the face of the waters." (Genesis 1:2b mg). It is a moving and meaningful picture of a great eagle looking for a place to nest and roost. Whether in the Tabernacle, or the Temple, the symbolism was the same; God was looking for His resting place, in which and from which, He could reveal His glory.

When the Lord Jesus was born, it was as if the purpose of God to have a dwelling place had been realised. For when Jesus was baptised, John the Baptist records that the Spirit of the

Lord came upon Him, never to leave Him (see John 1:32–33). The Lord Jesus, when challenged by the Jews in the Temple, had declared: "Destroy this temple, and in three days I will raise it up. He was claiming that He was the House of God, the Temple of the Living God, the Dwelling Place of the Living God (see John 2:19 cp. v. 22)." It is therefore of great significance that when we come to the last chapter of the Bible, we hear the word of the Holy Spirit: "The Spirit and the bride say, Come (Revelation 22:17a)." The Holy Spirit finally presents the result of all His work and endeavour—the Bridegroom and the bride in an eternal union and communion as the New Jerusalem, the eternal dwelling place of God.

The Lord Jesus as the Word of God, the Alpha and the Omega

The Lord Jesus is the Word of God. He is the unknown and unarticulated mind and heart of God revealed and articulated. What we could never have seen or understood, God the Father has made known in and through Him.

The Lord Jesus said: "I am the Alpha and the Omega, the first and the last, the beginning and the end." (Revelation 22:13). He is the whole alphabet of God. In other words, He is the language of God, the language through which God reveals Himself to us. By seeing the Lord Jesus we see the Father; by hearing the Messiah Jesus we hear God. The Almighty has communicated all of His heart and mind through Jesus. He is the light of the world. When we follow Him fully, we have the light of His life (see John 1:1–5 cp. v.14; 8:12).

The Approachable Godhead in the Lord Jesus

The amazing fact is that the Lord Jesus, the revelation of God the Father, was never distant, impersonal or unapproachable. Little children were always spontaneously drawn to Him, sometimes to the distress of the twelve disciples! Publicans and sinners loved Him! Far from feeling uncomfortable with Him, they were attracted to Him. Prostitutes, social outcasts, and lepers, all had the same experience. They did not feel uncomfortable in His Presence. So amazing was this attraction of the unsaved world to the Lord Jesus, that the Pharisees accused him of being: "a gluttonous man and a drunkard, a friend of tax-gatherers and sinners!" (Matthew 11:19b NASB). Whilst this description of the Lord Jesus is utterly wrong, it reveals the simple fact that the unsaved world did not find the Lord Jesus unapproachable, distant, or removed from their condition.

It reveals that the Father was totally at home in the Lord Jesus, and people of all sorts were drawn to Him. The heart of God—His Character and His Being—were expressed through Christ. The world in its worst state—homeless and destined for hell, derelict and ravaged by sin—was irresistibly drawn to Jesus. This He did without ever compromising His holiness and His purity. He lived for thirty-three years without ever sinning, though tempted in all points as we are (see Hebrews 4:15 cp. II Corinthians 5:21).

In the same manner in which the Father expressed and revealed Himself through the Messiah, the Lord Jesus desires to express and reveal Himself through the church. This was the lesson we learnt!

The Lampstand All of Gold

As the Holy Spirit concludes the sixty-five books of the Bible in one final book, He gathers up all the revelation and insight in a consummate manner. The last book is entitled: *The Revelation of Jesus Christ* (Revelation 1:1). The original Greek word is *"apokalupsis"* and means "unveiling," "disclosure," or "revelation." The manner in which this final book is entitled has to be for us believers, in the last phase of world history, vitally and strategically important. The apostle John, in a forced labour camp, sees the risen glorified Messiah in the midst of seven golden lampstands (see Revelation 1:12—16). They are clearly identified as seven churches in time and in specific localities (see Revelation 1:11). In Hebrew numerology the number seven signifies completeness or fullness. In other words, it is to the whole church of God from that day to this to whom the Lord Jesus, the Head of the church, is speaking.

Is the Lampstand the Lampstand of the Tabernacle and Temple?

From all the furniture of the Tabernacle and the Temple, the Holy Spirit took the seven-branched golden lampstand to represent the spiritual meaning and significance of the House of God (see Zechariah 4). It is clear that the lampstand which Zechariah saw in that vision was all to do with the building of the House of God—the building of it from its foundation to the top stone. In Zechariah's day, we may add, it was completed through much conflict and battle, and so it will be with us!

In my estimation it would be very strange if what had signified the House of God and its rebuilding in the Old Testament should not be used in the final book of the Bible. After all, it is noteworthy that there is in the sixty-six books of the Bible an incredible unity of symbolism and of figure. Moreover, the Head of the church was putting His finger on matters to do with its building up, and its completion, whilst also defining the problems which could cause paralysis and even the destruction of it all.

The Hebrew used for lampstand in Zechariah 4:2 is *Menorah,* and it is the seven-branched golden lampstand of the Tabernacle and Temple. In the Septuagint, the ancient Greek translation of the Old Testament, that lampstand in Zechariah 4:2 is translated by the Greek word *Luchnia.* This is the same Greek word used in Revelation 1:12. Therefore it seems clear that the lampstands, which represent seven churches in the first three chapters of the Apocalypse, the last book of the Bible, are the same as the menorah of Zechariah chapter 4, and of the Tabernacle and the Temple!

Jesus, the Light of the World and the Glory of God

The golden lampstand of the Tabernacle and the Temple was not merely a work of art. Its main use was to give light. Spiritually it represented the light and glory of God. In a very real way everything within the Tabernacle and the Temple represented the Lord Jesus. For example, to mention but a few of those items: The Golden Mercy Seat representing His finished work; there is no other place of mercy! The Golden Shewbread Table representing

Jesus as the Bread of Life and the continuous need to feed on Him daily; and The Golden Altar of Incense representing His continuous ministry of intercession without which we would fail.

The Testimony of Jesus

The Golden Lampstand represented the Lord Jesus as the light of the world and the outshining of the glory of God. The Messiah had said, as recorded by the apostle John: "I am the light of the world: he that followeth me shall not walk in the darkness, but shall have the light of life." (John 8:12b). John had already written: "And the Word became flesh, and dwelt among us (and we beheld His glory, glory as of the only begotten from the Father), full of grace and truth." (John 1:14).

The supreme testimony of the Lord Jesus was to be the language of God to mankind. It was the Godhead who spoke through the Lord Jesus, revealing God's Character and Being. As the Word of God, He bore testimony to the Eternal Purpose of God, and to the Authority, Inspiration, and Relevance of the written Word of God in its sixty-six books. In everything He did we see God as He truly is!

We could give two examples: The first is when the Lord Jesus, moved with compassion, actually touched a leper. It would have been the first time anyone had touched that leper since he had contracted leprosy (see Mark 1:40–41). It was a revelation of the kind of person God is and the kind of character God has. In fact it was God who touched him.

The second example is when a woman was taken in the act of adultery. The Scribes and Pharisees were seeking to try

Jesus, and brought her to Him rehearsing the Law of Moses: "Moses commanded us to stone such: what then sayest thou of her?" Jesus then said: "He that is without sin among you, let him first cast a stone at her." (see John 8:3—11). Beginning from the eldest, one by one they departed. The key to this act we find in the words: "What then sayest thou of her?" The Lord Jesus revealed the compassion, the mercy, and the love of God for that woman. He knew her background history and circumstances and acted accordingly.

All of this is contained in the term that the apostle Paul used when he wrote to Timothy that he should not be ashamed of *the testimony of our Lord* (see II Timothy 1:8). And again when he wrote to the church at Corinth about the testimony of Christ being confirmed in them (see I Corinthians 1:6). However, in the last book of the Bible the apostle John exclusively uses the term, *the testimony of Jesus* (see Revelation 1:2, 9; 12:17; 19:10; 20:4). It seems to me that we discover the key to our understanding of this term when we read Revelation 19: "I am a fellow-servant with thee and with thy brethren that hold the testimony of Jesus: worship God: for the testimony of Jesus is the spirit of prophecy." (10b). The testimony of Jesus is essentially prophetic. It is the forthtelling, the unveiling and revelation of God's heart and mind. When a church holds the testimony of Jesus, their life together becomes prophetic; it becomes a revelation of God to the world—the forthtelling of His thought and purpose.

The Testimony of Jesus and the Divine Building Programme

From the prophecy of Zechariah chapter 4, we discover that the symbolism of the golden lampstand is not only to do with Divine light and glory, but also with the building up and completion of the church. It was for this reason that it was used by the Holy Spirit in Revelation, chapters 1–3. For in exactly the same way as the golden lampstand holds the lamps with the oil alight, the church is "to hold the testimony of Jesus." If the testimony of Jesus is compromised or lost, the lampstand is removed from that congregation. Thus we have not only the encouragement of the risen Lord Jesus to the seven churches, but also His warnings that the testimony of Jesus could be removed. It should be obvious that if it is removed, the church has lost its essential function and calling to be God's home. Church history bears powerful witness to this fact.

Thou Hast Left Thy First Love

It is highly significant and noteworthy that the Head of the church warns one of the seven churches, the church in Ephesus:

> But I have this against thee, that thou didst leave thy first love. Remember therefore whence thou art fallen, and repent and do the first works; or else I come to thee, and will move thy lampstand out of its place, except thou repent (Revelation 2:4).

This is all the more remarkable since the risen glorified Lord commends the church in Ephesus for their works, their toil, their patience, their purity in doctrine, and their refusal to be taken in by some who falsely called themselves apostles.

The Messiah Jesus puts His finger on this question of "first love," as if it surpasses importance over anything else. First love is not puppy love, out of which we have grown since we were born again. It is a quality of love which leads to a total commitment to the Lord and to His purpose. It is the kind of love which underlies everything else. Once that quality of love is lost, everything becomes merely routine and dutiful. Our service has lost its heart. Nevertheless, it comes as a shock to us as believers that the Lord reacts with such severity.

Total First Love-the Explanation of the Whole Bible

A certain Jewish scribe once came to the Lord Jesus with a question:

> *What commandment is the first of all? Jesus answered: The first is, Hear, O Israel; The Lord our God, the Lord is one: and thou shalt **love the Lord thy God** with **all** thy heart, and with **all** thy soul, and with **all** thy mind, and with **all** thy strength. The second is this, Thou shalt **love thy neighbour** as thyself. There is none other commandment greater than these (Mark 12:28b—31 author's emphasis).*

Matthew in his record adds that Jesus had said:

On these two commandments the whole law
hangeth, and the prophets (Matthew 22:40).

To love the Lord with all your heart, all your soul, all your mind, and all your strength, and to love your neighbour as you love yourself, is the quality of first love. Out of your total love for the Lord, springs forth the loving of your neighbour. With such love all our worship, service, and care has meaning.

We see this also in the manner in which the apostle John concludes his gospel. The Gospel of John is different from the three synoptic gospels, Matthew, Mark and Luke. They record the facts, whereas the Gospel of John is an interpretation of the life and death of the Lord Jesus. The manner in which John concludes his record is extremely important. He emphasises that all our service and ministry must spring out of our first love for the Lord Jesus.

The risen Christ had met the apostles at the Lake of Galilee and had prepared for them a breakfast. At the end of that meal He asked Peter: "Lovest thou me more than these?" Jesus used the Greek word, *agape*, which means to "love with strong affection," to "love sacrificially and unselfishly." Such love leads to a total commitment and devotion to the Lord to being a living sacrifice. Peter, after his fall and denial of the Lord three times, could not rise to that level. He used the Greek word *Phileo*, which means "to be fond of," "to have affection," or "to be a friend." At the end of each of these three questionings of Peter, the Lord Jesus said: "Feed My lambs …, tend My sheep …, feed My sheep." From this we understand that the heart of genuine service has to be this "first love" (see John 21:12–17). Without it everything loses its meaning. Once we see this we begin to understand why the Lord treats the loss of first love with such severity. The light in the lampstand has dimmed and died, and the glory of God has departed. It is the story of so much in church history!

If, as we have repeatedly pointed out in this ninth chapter, the Lord looks for a resting place, a dwelling place, a home, it has no meaning without first love. When the Lord turned a restored and renovated Halford House into a warm home with a sense of "family," it became one more vital lesson. Can the homeless sinner ever find God in a cold, dutiful routine, however correct or true to the Word it may be? It is the love of God in the fellowship of saved human beings which overwhelms the sinner and brings them into a revelation of the love and mercy of God.

10.
The Experience of Corporate Prayer and Intercession

One of the main features of the fellowship of believers that met at Halford House was the emphasis on intercession and prayer. On every level of the work—whether it was the meeting of the elder brothers, the children's work, the evangelistic work, or the practical work in the house and garden—it all began with a time of prayer. It was more than a simple beginning word of prayer. It was an atmosphere that had developed through our knowing that in everything we needed the direction and the wisdom of the Lord. It was not routine and religious but seemed to develop naturally out of a desire that the Lord Jesus should be Lord and Head of every aspect of the life of the fellowship. Whenever we confronted problems, we would simply commit them to the Lord. Of course, the fellowship had been born in intercession and travail, and that had moulded its life and character.

Especial Times of Waiting upon the Lord

In the earlier years we often used to put aside the normal routine of meetings and spend a week in waiting upon the Lord. Nearly everyone would come to those times. They were incredibly refreshing and renewing. It seemed that the Lord used them to realign us to Himself and to His purpose. We never had any pattern for the week, but simply worshipped the Lord and waited upon Him. The Lord used those times to shape our course, to speak to us and to lead us practically.

Days of Prayer and Fasting

Sometimes we had days of prayer and fasting. Whilst these times were occasional, the Lord used them very greatly. For example: When the news reached us of the arrest by the Maoist authorities of Brother Watchman Nee in 1952, and the arrest of all the elders and workers in the many assemblies of believers all over China between 1954 to 1956, we had especial days of prayer and fasting. James Ma, a brother who had been present in Shanghai at the time of Brother Nee's arrest, had managed to escape from mainland China by swimming across the narrow sea to Hong Kong. He brought us an up to date account of all that was happening. We also had a very close relationship with Stephen and Mary Kaung, Elizabeth Fischbacher, Lena Barnes, and Miss Card, to name but a few. All had connections with the work in China.

We had a worldwide view and burdens concerning many areas of the world. They ranged from China to New Guinea and Indonesia, to Japan and Korea, to India, to Singapore and S.E. Asia, and to the continents of Africa and South America. We had a close relationship with Norman Grubb, the General Secretary of the Worldwide Evangelisation Crusade (WEC) and his successor Len Mowles. They gave us much knowledge and information about many areas of the world. They often came to us to minister and share information. This kept alive a burden for the Lord's work throughout the world. On occasion we prayed for Nepal through our connection with the Nepal Christian Fellowship, originally the Nepal Evangelistic Band, and particularly the leprosy work. We had close connection with India through Brother Bahkt Singh, Fred and Meg Flack, Ron and Evelyn Bissell, and others.

We prayed for Africa, especially for the Congo, and had much fellowship with the precious believers there through Willie F. B. Burton, Norman Grubb, Colin and Ina and Mary Rees, all of whom visited us many times at Halford. The Simba Rebellion and the resulting martyrdom of many believers in the Congo was the cause for such a day of prayer and fasting. We also had close connection with many other parts of Africa. In fact, at one point, we had a small group of Nigerian and Ghanaian brothers who fellowshipped with us and gave us further insight.

On another occasion we had a visit from a German brother who had worked very much in Indonesia. He was a tall, well-built, blond-haired German. He told us how the Lord had led him to Timor at the beginning of the Timor Revival. Apparently, an old unsaved chieftain was given a vision of a tall, well-built, blond-haired, blue-eyed man. The man the chieftain had seen in the vision, so he said, would come to the tribe with a message which they had never before heard. He told everyone, wherever the chieftain went, that they should be careful to listen to the message this blond-haired white man would bring them when he came. The result was that when this missionary did come, the Lord had already prepared the ground, and whole tribes turned to the Lord. This led us to pray with much burden for Indonesia, for Timor and for New Guinea.

We often prayed for the salvation of Israel. In the beginning of the fellowship we had much connection with Jordan, through Dr. Henry and Ruth Backhouse who went out to the Middle East from us. After 1967 and the Six Day War, those areas in which they were working became part of Israel. Thus, Israel became a growing burden for intercession.

There were many other parts of the world for which we had real burdens and prayed. We have not mentioned them, but the relationship to them was just as real. I have written all of this to show that although we were a small company of mainly young people, we were not bound to our own problems and needs. The Lord turned our hearts toward the whole world.

The Prayer and Bible Weeks

This worldwide burden was greatly reinforced by the holding of Prayer and Bible Weeks from time to time at Halford House. These especial times were led by two very dear brothers, Dennis Clark and Alec Buchanan. Dennis had been used of the Lord to found not only Intercessors for Britain, but many other national intercessor groups. He had a gift for discerning what the Holy Spirit was pinpointing in national and international situations. As a result, genuine intercession was focused. It often rose to a crescendo until the burden would turn into praise and worship.

The situations prayed for in those times had been settled by the Lord's intervention. This taught us as a fellowship much about the character of intercession and the need to be focused.

Alec Buchanan was also a remarkable personality. He had suffered much from an accident in his youth. During the Blitz, when his home was bombed, he fell and seriously gashed his head on a solid iron mantle piece. He was rushed to the hospital to be operated upon in the midst of an air raid. The power in the hospital was continually being cut by the bombardment, and the surgeon basically gave up, believing that the patient would die anyway. In fact, the result was that miraculously Alec survived against all odds. However, it left him with many serious problems with his sight and his hearing. This, in turn, instead of embittering him made him an incredibly sensitive and thoughtful individual. Once the Lord fully possessed him, He gifted him in many ways. Those who heard Alec's prophetic utterances will never forget them. These utterances were mainly related to individuals or to assemblies of believers, but not to national or international matters. Again and again, it seemed as if, spiritually, he saw through people. I was often amazed when he prophesied over a person I knew well; it was as if he saw everything about them. Many times the Lord put His finger on a situation in a person's life, and that person was transformed. It gave me a new understanding of the Biblical prophet as a seer.

These Prayer and Bible Weeks often transformed the attitude of many of those who attended them. Those times brought us into an understanding of the manner in which the Holy Spirit illuminates the Word of God and through that Word transforms us. They also taught us much about the nature of intercession and of prayer warfare, and the essential need of covering whilst being engaged in them.

The Main Weekly Time of Prayer

The main time of prayer in the fellowship at Halford House was always on a Tuesday evening. It was well attended and often exciting. Indeed, young people, not long saved, would come to the prayer meeting instead of the Bible study because at times it was so thrilling. This was especially the case when we prayed for national situations. Often they went home after the meeting and switched on the television to see if our prayers had been answered!

These times became an instruction to all of us in the ways of the Lord. It was not only to do with national situations but also local situations. We all had to exercise faith in the practical work of the restoration and renovation of Halford House. It was not only for finances but for the many practical problems which confronted the actual work of recovery. Sometimes those problems seemed insoluble, if not at times impossible! We experienced the answers to our intercession and grew in the Lord. For all of the fellowship it became a teaching manual of the Holy Spirit. Indeed we kept a prayer book each week for the matters which were suggested for prayer and where we also recorded the answers. It was remarkable that every main event in the practical work of restoration and recovery seemed to come to a crisis of decision on a Tuesday.

The Salient Features of the Prayer Ministry at the Halford House

It would be good to underline the salient features of the prayer ministry at Halford House. It was the Lord who formed the prayer ministry which then gave rise to certain characteristics.

The first characteristic was a sense of expectancy. We had witnessed so many remarkable answers to prayer, ranging from small matters to large. It was this which gave rise to an expectancy that the Lord would hear and answer prayer.

The second characteristic was the manner in which so many learned to discern the anointing in the prayer meeting and to follow it. This is absolutely essential for a "successful" prayer meeting. I mean by successful, the fact that the Lord heard our prayer and answered it. The anointing is basically the leadership of the Holy Spirit. To discern the leadership of the Holy Spirit in prayer or intercession requires an education and a training by Him. Here the old saying is so apt, "Prayer is not taught; it is caught!" We often learn how to discern the anointing and leadership of the Holy Spirit and follow Him by being with others who had already learned to discern it.

The third characteristic was learning what to do when at some point in the prayer time we lost the anointing! When a session of prayer is derailed either by sentiment, emotion, or manipulation, it is not corrected by barging back to the original flow. It comes by all of us looking to the Lord to bring us back to the anointing. The anointing in that time of prayer had been lost through the flesh at work; it is not regained by using the flesh. Furthermore, a time of prayer where the Lord fulfils His purpose is not when everything is "pattern perfect," but when we learn how to get back on track. This is part of the warfare of prayer, and learning to overcome the Enemy's attempts to foil effective prayer.

The fourth characteristic was to learn to exercise living faith. We learnt that such faith cannot come from the flesh. It is a work of the Holy Spirit to stir up faith in us. At times it can be the spiritual gift of faith manifested in the time of prayer. So often, living faith is expressed in the declaration and proclamation of the Word of God in any given situation or problem. God given faith expressed by one believer is often "infectious" and spreads to others.

The fifth characteristic was learning, by the Spirit, to second one another's prayer. There is an idea amongst those who are part of a prayer ministry that once a matter is mentioned by one prayer warrior there is no need for further prayer. We learnt, on the contrary, that a matter has to be established in the mouth of two or three witnesses (see II Corinthians 13:1). Therefore, the Holy Spirit will lead other prayer warriors to second or to agree in prayer with what has been previously prayed. In fact this is the idea or concept behind saying, "Amen."

The sixth characteristic was how to learn to discern the will of God in order to intercede. Genuine intercession begins with the knowledge of the will of God in any given circumstance. Once we know what the will of God is in fellowship with the Lord we pray it into being. We learnt that this is contained in the pattern prayer which the Lord gave us: "Thy kingdom come. Thy will be done, as in heaven, so on earth" (Matthew 6:10). Once the will of God in any situation we were facing had been revealed to us, the Lord taught us to make a declaration; we should proclaim that His throne and Kingdom would enter our circumstances and His will be fulfilled in them, as in heaven, so on earth.

The seventh characteristic was to learn how by faith and patience we inherit the promises. When the Lord reveals His will concerning any situation, a huge battle develops. Satan cannot abide the will of God being fulfilled! We have to learn that there are times of prayer when the Lord answers instantly and fulfils His purpose. When that happens we praise the Lord with full hearts! Nevertheless, so often we have to wait for months or even years and sometimes decades before it is fulfilled. It is then that we need not only faith but patience. The writer of the Hebrew letter writes: "That ye be not sluggish, but imitators of them who through faith and patience inherit the promises." (Hebrews 6:12).

A good example of faith and **patience** is the story of the Red Cross Hut. It was a corrugated tin hut that was permitted to be placed on the ground belonging to Halford House at the beginning of the First World War (1914–1918). It was to be used by the Red Cross and to be removed at the end of that war! In fact, it was never removed! It not only remained through the years from 1919 until 1939 but right through the Second World War (1939–1945). It was still there when we bought Halford House in 1954! The hut was a dreadful "eyesore." It was less than four metres from our windows. Over few other matters was there as much sustained prayer as over the Red Cross hut! However nothing ever happened!

I was living in Jerusalem, the Lord having called me to Israel in 1977. Years later the miracle took place. The Red Cross approached Halford House with the offer of the hut. I only know that the fellowship had their own real experience of the Lord intervening and finally answering all those years of prayer. The Lord answered with a miracle which encompassed the whole fellowship. It was not only faith that had been exercised but also patience.

The eighth characteristic was our understanding that one did not have to use special "prayer language" in prayer. Whilst we should always be reverent and remember that it is the Lord with whom we are talking, we do not have to bore the Lord by the most unnatural, abnormal kind of tone, voice, or theatrics. We can be absolutely normal and "natural" in our approach to prayer and intercession. I think it would be fair to say that the prayer at Halford was generally speaking natural and normal. The only problem we had was whether the voice could be heard. Therefore we asked people to speak up.

Why should our speaking with the Lord be unnatural and theatrical? There is, however, an obvious need to hear the prayer. Nevertheless, in expressing our petitions, in our beseeching, or in our enquiring there is no need for the unnatural! What is the Lord to do when we have a façade? First of all, the façade has to be pierced if the Lord is to reach the real person.

'Be in the Sandwiches!'

Sometimes the believer at prayer was too natural! I remember the first time Eileen Hillier, a Cockney woman, ever spoke in prayer at Halford. She had not long been saved. It was in a prayer time for an evangelistic outreach. We called this kind of meeting a "squash" because you squeezed everyone in! We had suggested that the Lord should be in everything to do with that time. The Lord Jesus should be in the meeting, in the testimonies which would be given, in the solo, in the music, and in the serving of refreshments. Dear Eileen launched forth, having never prayed before publicly. She prayed as she normally talked: "Lord, be in the testimonies, be in the solo, be in the music, be in the giving out of refreshments, and Lord, be in the sandwiches!!" She was going to help make the sandwiches. I am sure the Lord understood her prayer, but everyone tried not to laugh! However, you could hear the sounds of stifled laughter everywhere.

The Nun from Uganda

Another instance was over a nun who had been coming to us for a number of Sunday mornings. She was dressed as a nun and was a black African from Uganda. I noticed that on the four consecutive Sunday mornings she came, she had received the bread and the wine during the Lord's Table. I was intrigued and shaking hands with people at the front door as they left, I said to her how glad I was that she was coming. She replied that she found the Catholic Church further up Richmond Hill very dead! She said she had heard about Halford House and decided to come. Then she said: "I am so thrilled with it; it is exactly the same as our times in Uganda." I told the prayer meeting about this and said that we should pray for her and for other Catholics.

One of our ex-borstal boys ventured forth in prayer with an unforgettable petition. He prayed: "Lord, we thank you so much for that black nun who so appreciates our fellowship. We pray that you will use her to bring all the monks from the monastery to our meeting and save them!" We all had visions of this dear nun with a single file of monks trailing behind her, coming to the meeting!

The Four Months and the Four Years of Intercession

The work of the Lord at Halford House was born out of much travail and prayer beginning on the first day of September 1951. It had all begun with a burden which the Holy Spirit had placed upon a few of us. We had covenanted to seek the Lord about this burden until it was fulfilled. That led to Koinonia, and then to the Community Centre, and finally the Astor Club before the purchase of Halford House. The whole fellowship, as I have already written, was much influenced and moulded by those four months of intense intercession with which it all began.

Ten Years to the Day

Ten years later to the day on the 1st of September 1961, the fellowship of believers at Halford House began to pray not only for the Thames valley but for the world in general! By then we had come to understand certain principles and features about the church. It was a great concern to us that most Christians seemed to understand the word *church* as having to do with a physical building. It was somewhere you left by mistake your purse, your umbrella, or your Bible! It was hardly ever understood to be a company of saved men and women. The term, *Head and body* used extensively in the New Testament, was rarely used amongst Christians. The burden we had was that the Lord would break down this impenetrable wall of ignorance, breaking it wide open for the truth and the reality of the church to be known in a living way.

Prayer for the Recovery of the Truth of the Church as the Body of Christ

We understood that the Holy Spirit had recovered many truths beginning for example with the "Authority, Inspiration and Relevance of the Word of God," and "Justification by Faith alone" in the Reformation; the truth of "Believers Baptism" with the general Baptists and Congregationalists, the Anabaptists and the Mennonites; "the New Birth" in the First Great Awakening with John and Charles Wesley and George Whitfield; the recovery of the "Unity of all Believers" and the "Second Coming of The Lord" with the Brethren; "the Reality and Necessity of the Work of the Holy Spirit and the Spiritual Gifts," the "Emphasis on His Anointing and His Fullness" with the Pentecostal Awakening. Now the burden we felt was that the Lord would recover the truth concerning the "Church as the Body of Christ of which He is Head."

We had a burden from the Lord for a mighty breakthrough in this matter which would bring millions to Christ. At first it was just a general feeling that one or two of us carried. As we fellowshipped about it, it became ever more clear that we had to set everything aside and seek the Lord. Once we became sure that it was the Lord who was burdening us, we began to meet for prayer. It is an interesting fact that not one of us noticed that it was ten years previously to the day when we had started praying daily. That had lasted four months and had resulted in the fellowship. It was not until a week or two after we had commenced praying that we suddenly realised that fact.

Now we were united that we had to seek the Lord whatever the cost. Thus we began intense intercession on September 1st 1961. As a result we put aside all the usual meetings, except the Lord's Table on Sunday morning, and the evangelistic meeting on Sunday evening. Instead, we would use the after time of that meeting for prayer.

The Four Years Prayer Meeting

We began a prayer meeting which was to last four years. Only the Lord could have sustained this prayer. We prayed for all areas of the world, for the salvation of the unsaved, and the spiritual growth of believers. We prayed in particular that this wall of ignorance, blindness and prejudice concerning the church—its nature, its life, and its function—should be destroyed. The first year of prayer and intercession was lively, as was the second and third. By the end of the first year of intercession a number of people had been saved amongst us. It became a concern that these new believers had no teaching other than Sunday morning after the Lord's Table. So we sought the Lord as to what we should do. As a result we felt the Lord directing us to restore the Bible study on Thursday evening, and this we did.

The Breakthrough in the Third Year of Prayer

Toward the end of the third year we began to flag but carried on by faith through His grace and power. It came to a head on a Wednesday. On that evening it was the smallest number we ever had in the whole three years. For one reason or another all the main prayer warriors seemed not to be there. I thought to myself, I ought to speak with Eric Luck, one of the elders and the pianist at the meeting, as to whether we were not "flogging a dead horse."

Suddenly in the middle of that evening it was as if we looked into heaven. I shall never forget it! It had been the most boring, dull, heavy prayer time that I could remember in all those three years. One could almost describe it as dead! But as I have said, all of a sudden the whole time changed. It was as if eternal things suddenly became absolute reality. We all became very lively, almost hysterical; some were laughing. Then a believer began to praise the Lord, and then another, until the whole time turned into worship and praise. It was as if we were seeing the Lord Himself in our midst. As we were worshipping the Lord, almost out of our bodies, Muriel Western uttered the words, "Within a year the wall will come down." It was based upon a Scripture she had just read quietly to herself and which she felt was for us all. Everyone in that time witnessed to it. Then the evening turned into a period of intense worship and praise. From being the dullest, heaviest, boring and least attended meeting we had in three years, it became a time of faith and worship. Looking back I realised that it was the Enemy who had planned to make that evening impossible. As usual Satan was using a heavy blanket of death to render any breakthrough impossible. The Lord, however, turned it into victory.

A Year of Worship and Praise

All of us felt that the Lord had met us and that He had heard our prayer and was about to move. We did not feel we could go on interceding since we felt the Lord had heard and answered. It was thus that we decided we should continue to meet each evening, but only for worship and praise. We had wonderful times.

It was around this point that we first heard of the manner in which the Holy Spirit had fallen on a meeting in an old Methodist church in Cornwall. It had resulted in many being born again and filled with the Spirit. Others were delivered and healed. To our amazement many of them spoke in tongues. Then almost at the same time we heard of a meeting in South-West Wales where the same awakening and revival took place with the same results! Almost simultaneously, we heard of yet another meeting in North-East England where the Holy Spirit fell on a whole congregation. As we worshipped and praised the Lord, we felt we were seeing the first signs of answers to our prayers.

A Huge Uncontained Flood of the Holy Spirit

Before long what had been a stream became a huge flood which could not be contained. From all sides we began to hear of the most amazing conversions, healings, deliverances, and the manifestation of the gifts of the Holy Spirit. I remember one incident when the minister of a small mission in Putney, that had not seen a baptism for decades, began to see conversions, healings, deliverances, baptisms, and much else. It all began when he was taking the dog for a walk on Putney common. He suddenly felt weak around the knees, saw a bench and went to sit on it. Almost immediately, he threw his head back and began to speak in a tongue. He was filled with the Holy Spirit. He had never had anything to do with Pentecostals or Pentecostal teaching. His dog sat there looking at him as if he was mad! He decided to return home, only to find that in their kitchen his wife had experienced the exact same visitation of the Holy Spirit.

On another occasion there was a ring at the door at Halford House, and there was a missionary from Nepal, whom I had known since I was in my teens. She had always treated me as if she was an older sister seeking to put me right. She said, "Have you got any time for a spot of fellowship?" Before that time she would never have said anything like that. I took one look at her and knew that the Holy Spirit had met her. I said, "Have you had an experience of the Holy Spirit?" She replied, "How did you know?" It was obvious; she radiated the Presence of the Lord.

The Worldwide Charismatic Renewal and Revival

It was clear to all of us that something tremendous was happening. Before long we heard of renewing and reviving everywhere— all over Europe, through Scandinavia, the Netherlands, Germany, and France. I should make it clear at this point that I am not saying that our years of prayer had led to the great Charismatic Renewal and Revival which swept over the whole world. There must have been others in different parts of the world also praying for such a breakthrough. The Charismatic Renewal brought millions to Christ, whilst at the same time bringing millions of Christians into a new living experience of the Lord Jesus by the Holy Spirit. It had renewed the emphasis upon a real experience of the Holy Spirit and of His gifts. For the first time we heard people speaking of the Church as the Body of the Lord Jesus. It brought a new understanding of the church as the Spiritual House of the Lord built up with living stones.

In the fellowship at Halford House we felt a deep sense of fulfilment that a burden which had come from the Holy Spirit had been discharged. Sadly, much of the Charismatic has now become a denomination as real as any other. It is a fact that every initiative which our Lord has launched by the Holy Spirit since Pentecost has within a few generations become a denomination. In those few generations the Lord has swept millions into His Kingdom, brought the believers back to the original principles, and turned nations upside down, transforming them and setting His purpose forward in the recovery of original truth. Certainly, in its beginnings the Charismatic Revival was an overwhelming power of the Lord sweeping all before it into the Kingdom.

A.B Simpson's Prophetic Words

I remember an occasion when Brother Sparks told me of a time of fellowship he had with A.B. Simpson. Mr. Sparks was a young man in his twenties and was on a first visit to the United States. There were three well known Christian ministers he wanted to see and hear—they were A.T. Pierson, A.J. Gordon, and A.B. Simpson. Brother Sparks went to different places to hear these brothers and was particularly impressed and blessed by A.B. Simpson. He asked if he could have an interview with A.B. Simpson and it was arranged. During that time Mr. Sparks asked him what he thought about the end of the age, and what would be any special feature for the Lord's people. A.B. Simpson thought for a while and then said, "There will be a new discovery worldwide of the Person and the Work of the Holy Spirit. Nothing else will carry the Lord's people through the last phase of world history and into the coming of the Kingdom of God."

11.
One Body in Christ

The Organic Nature of the Church

The Oxford Dictionary defines the word *Organic*, amongst other meanings, as being "characterised by continuous and natural development." The apostle Paul many times writes of the Church as being "the body of our Lord." In the Old Testament the House of the Lord—whether the Tabernacle or the Temple—was never described in that manner. Even in the four Gospels the church is not referred to in this way. The physical body of the Lord Jesus, of course, is mentioned as well as His own reference to His body being the Temple of the Lord (see John 2:19—22).

It is clear that when the Lord Jesus appeared to Saul of Tarsus and saved him, it had a tremendous impact on Saul. From that meeting the apostle Paul was given an understanding of the church as the body of the Messiah. The Lord had said to Saul: "Saul, Saul, why persecutest thou me?" (Acts 9:4b). Saul could well have reacted by saying, "I am not persecuting You, but Your followers!" He was in fact hounding Messianic believers to death.

On reflection and by revelation, Paul understood that to touch a Messianic Jew or a Christian was touching the Lord Jesus Himself. That was the beginning of Saul's understanding that Christ and those He saved were one entity! It was this revelation by the Holy Spirit which brought Paul into his understanding of the church as the body of Christ.

We see this in the many references in the apostle Paul's letters to Christ as the Head and the church as His body. For example:

For even as we have many members in one body,
and all the members have not the same office: so we,
who are many, are one body in Christ, and severally
members one of another (Romans 12:4—5).

Or again:

For as the body is one, and hath many members, and all
the members of the body, being many, are one body; so also
is Christ. For in one Spirit were we all baptized into one
body, whether Jews or Greeks, whether bond or free, and
were all made to drink of one Spirit. For the body is not one
member, but many… Now ye are the body of Christ, and
severally members thereof (1 Corinthians 12:12—14, 27).

And again:

But speaking truth in love, may grow up in all things into

him, who is the head, even Christ; from whom all the body
fitly framed and knit together through that which every
joint supplieth, according to the working in due measure
of each several part, maketh the increase of the body unto
the building up of itself in love (Ephesians 4:15—16).

Furthermore:

And he is the head of the body, the church: who is the
beginning, the firstborn from the dead; that in all things
he might have the preeminence (Colossians 1:18).

It is patently clear that the apostle Paul did not see the church as a religious organisation or institution, but as a living, organic entity joined to its Head enthroned at the right hand of the Majesty on high. The church was and is in an essential unity with the risen, ascended and glorified Lord Jesus. Paul recognised the Head and the body as being one organic entity. When the Lord Jesus as the Head of the body is given the pre-eminence in any fellowship of believers, the Holy Spirit is able to communicate the mind and thoughts of the Head to the body. In this way the Head makes known the will of God and gives practical direction, making available the grace, the power, and the wisdom needed to walk in obedience to that direction.

In Practice It Began at Pentecost

When the ascended glorified Messiah poured out the Holy Spirit at Pentecost, 120 saved human beings became 120 members of a body whose Head was at the right hand of the Father. This had never before happened in the history of the universe. This "Head and body" was not physical but a spiritual reality. It was an organic entity as real as the actual union between a physical head and body! Those 120 ordinary believers, many whose names we do not even know, were destined to turn the whole Jewish world upside down. In the end they were to triumph even over the Roman Empire. Within hours there were 3,120 saved human beings, within weeks 5,000, and many more within a few more months. Without any evangelistic organisation or advertisement, or all the usual paraphernalia we consider essential to church growth, they not only grew in grace and power, but were empowered to overcome the world around them. The price they paid was enormous, for they died in their thousands as martyrs.

To begin with they were only Messianic Jews. The Holy Spirit then brought in the Samaritans, overcoming all the hostility and hatred between the Jews and the Samaritans. They became one family in the Lord Jesus. Even more remarkable was the bringing in of the Gentiles. It began in a Roman Officer's home in Caesarea, and was destined to reach the ends of the earth. The great divide between Jew and Gentile had not merely been bridged but had been abolished, and a New Man produced!

The Intelligence Normally Centered in the Head

Whilst the new born church owned the Lord as its Head, heard and obeyed Him, it was invincible and unbeatable. Nothing on earth, in heaven, or in hell, could stop the purpose of God being fulfilled. The only way in which Satan and his host could frustrate that purpose of God was to drive a wedge between the church and its Head. Once the enemy could achieve that objective, the church would become something other than what it was destined to be. After all, the intelligence is normally centred in the head, although with some I have my doubts! The fact that the Lord Jesus is called "the Head" must have something to do with the will of God, with His intelligence and direction of the body. It is the understanding of the will of God and His ability to direct the body which makes all the difference between growth and paralysis. It therefore becomes clear that hearing the Lord, discerning His will, and obeying His direction is vital; it is all important. The Holy Spirit jealously guards this "organic" connection of the body with the Head; for it will always result in the continuous and natural development of the church.

The Word of God Increased

The manner in which the book of Acts records the growth of the early church is noteworthy: "And the word of God increased; and the number of the disciples multiplied in Jerusalem exceedingly; and a great company of the priests were obedient to the faith (Acts 6:7)." And again: "But the word of God grew and multiplied (Acts 12:24)." Or again: "So mightily grew the word of the Lord and prevailed (Acts 19:20)."

We may well ask how the Word of God increases, grows and multiplies; how it grew and prevailed. The Canon of Scripture is the Word of God; we cannot add to it or multiply it or subtract from it, deleting areas within it. Those references must refer to the believers, the members of the body of Christ, in whom the implanted Word of the Lord took root, grew, and prevailed, not only in their personal lives and their family life, but also in the life of the church.

Everything Develops from the Organic Nature of the Church

Out of this organic nature of the church everything develops. We are one body in Christ and members one of another. The apostle Paul speaks of being a joint of supply (see Ephesians 4:16). Such a healthy joint receives and contributes. In this manner the whole body increases and is built up; it functions as a normal body should function. When something is blocked in any joint of the body, the whole body suffers. The priesthood of all believers is, therefore, of enormous importance to the health of the church. This vital truth needs not only to be honoured, but place needs to be given for its practice.

How We Came to Recognise the Priesthood of All Believers

In the same manner as most Evangelical believers, we at Halford House believed in the Priesthood of all Believers. However we did not practise it. Some of our leading brothers would meet together before the main meetings and seek to find the Lord's mind for them. We would then arrange the order of the meeting, designating different leading brothers to take responsibility for either its beginning or its development. Our general feeling was that you could not have a completely open meeting, where any "Tom, Dick and Harry, or Ethel, Eileen and Edna" could contribute! The idea filled us with horror!

It was Elizabeth Fischbacher whom the Lord used to change our understanding and to lead us into a much deeper and fuller way. She was the missionary nearest to Watchman Nee. This dear sister was visiting us and she asked Margaret and I how things were going in the fellowship. I told her about the question we had over the practice of the Priesthood of all Believers. She commented on how vital and strategic to the growth of the church the Priesthood of all Believers is. Then, fixing her blue eyes on me, she said: "Are you not able to trust the Holy Spirit over this matter? Is it only safe if it is under your control? Surely it is more than absolutely safe when the Holy Spirit is in charge!" It was like a thunder bolt! Suddenly I saw the situation in its real light; it was surely safer to trust the Holy Spirit than to trust man.

I took the whole matter to the fellowship for prayer. After seeking the Lord we became of one mind that from this point onwards we would trust the Holy Spirit. As a result there are four matters it would be good to underline.

Firstly, the whole church grew in grace and in the knowledge of the Lord Jesus as a result.

Secondly, we multiplied almost immediately in numbers.

Thirdly, it was amazing the way the Holy Spirit led our open times, especially at the Lord's Table. Each Sunday it was the Lord who led us, unfolding a truth without any human management! That in itself became a blessing to the whole fellowship.

Fourthly, in my recollection in something like thirty years we only had to silence someone twice. We discovered that it was indeed safer to trust the Holy Spirit.

Lastly, a fellowship or assembly of believers must have strong spiritual and recognised leaders in order to practise the Priesthood of All Believers

The Fellowship of the Church

Furthermore, this is the meaning of genuine fellowship. The Greek word *Koinonia* means to "have something in common," "to be partners," simply to "share." We share one Head, one Lord, one Saviour; we share His one salvation and we share His resurrection life. We also share one body. Fellowship covers not only our meetings together but our life as a community. We are to love one another, to care for one another, and to uphold one another. It is this kind of love and concern for one another which becomes a testimony to the world around us. The open times we had at Halford House were fellowship in action.

The Mistake We Made in the False Appointment of Elders and Deacons

We learnt the organic nature of the church through a mistake we made. As a fellowship of believers, due to our ignorance, we appointed elders and deacons. We saw it as a "Biblical pattern," and we believed it was obedience to the Word of God. This was in the very early days before we had purchased Halford House. We have already mentioned this in chapter two. Of course many of us had a Baptist or Congregationalist background, and we were influenced by the practice of those denominations. However, we began to see that the people we had appointed elders and deacons did not have the spiritual character or maturity required. At the same time we had also noticed those who had the anointing required for leadership.

We really did not know what to do, but began to seek the Lord together. It was a situation fraught with the danger of division and faction. The mistake we had made, as we have said, was due to our total ignorance of the organic nature of the church. It was not due to self-seeking on the part of those who had been appointed elders and deacons. Once we all recognised that we had made a mistake, the way was clear for us to seek the Lord for His mind on the subject. It was in this way that we came to recognise the organic nature of the church—the spiritual development of those whom the Lord would appoint to hold any kind of office in it.

It is recorded of the apostle Paul and those brothers who were traveling with him, that it was on their return journey to Antioch when they laid hands on certain brothers and appointed them elders in all the churches:

And when they had appointed for them elders in every
church, and had prayed with fasting, they commended them
to the Lord, on whom they had believed (Acts 14:23).

This meant that they had given time for spiritual growth and maturity to develop in the brothers who were appointed elders. We should carefully note that Paul, in particular, with his apostleship and wisdom could have appointed elders on the first part of his journey. However, they had left time for the brothers to grow and for their gift to be recognised by the church they were in. It is clear that the apostle did not believe that he could appoint elders without the recognition of the believers in the fellowship concerned.

It was also for this reason that Paul had left Titus in Crete to appoint elders in every city (see Titus 1:5). He could have appointed them at the beginning with prayer and fasting. However, he left Titus in Crete to allow more time for the development of spiritual growth and character. We have the same idea when Paul wrote: "Lay hands hastily on no man." (1 Timothy 5:22a). It is worth noting that Paul insisted on time being given for spiritual growth and maturity. To appoint elders or deacons suddenly or too early could damage the growth in the person concerned or harm that fellowship of believers.

As a fellowship we had learnt a vital lesson. It was not only related to the recognition of elders and deacons, but it covered a whole number of aspects of church life—the appointment of those working with children, with youth, in evangelistic work or other areas in the local work of the Lord. The lesson we learnt was that we needed to be sure of the spiritual life and growth of those who were being appointed to different positions. So often it required a little more time for a person to grow and mature. To recognise a believer too early would always damage their growth to maturity.

The Unity of the Spirit

The enemy has not only ferociously attacked the organic nature of the church, but also the oneness of the body with the Head, and the oneness of the members of the body with one another. Satan and his hierarchy have clearly understood that the only way to frustrate the purpose and the will of God is to destroy the organic nature of the church and its essential unity. The history of the church bears ample witness to this fact. Every initiative the Head of the church has taken has been sidetracked. Nevertheless, the Lord Jesus has not been defeated. The fact that He has taken these repeated initiatives in the recovery and restoration of the church reveals that in the end He intends to win! Therefore we should not be downcast and demoralised but should become overcomers by His grace. With Him we are on the victory side! All that we need to be winners with Him, He has made available to us.

Give Diligence to Keep the Unity of the Spirit

We should carefully note the manner in which, by the Holy Spirit, the apostle writes to the church at Ephesus. He beseeches them:

> To walk worthily of the calling wherewith ye were called, with all lowliness and meekness, with longsuffering, forbearing one another in love; giving diligence to **keep** the unity of the Spirit in the bond of peace (Ephesians 4:1b—3 author's emphasis).

Mark and underline the word *keep*. You cannot keep something you do not possess. Once you have a house you can maintain it; once you have a dog you can keep it. To keep or to maintain the Unity of the Spirit means that we have already been born of God **into that Unity** and we need to maintain it. In fact, once we have been saved we have been repositioned by God. Whereas, before we were in the world, we are now in Christ. For example:

*There is therefore now no condemnation to them that are **in Christ Jesus** (Romans 8:1).*

And again:

*But of him are ye **in Christ Jesus**, who was made unto us wisdom from God, and righteousness and sanctification, and redemption (1 Corinthians 1:30).*

Or again:

*Wherefore if any man is **in Christ**, there is a new creation (II Corinthians 5:17 mg author's emphasis).*

The revelation by the Spirit of God that we have been repositioned in Christ by the Father is a glorious truth. It opens up the whole New Testament, and everything given to us in Christ. It is summed up in the words of the Lord Jesus: "Abide in me, and I in you." (John 15:4a).

In fact, to be "in Christ" is to be also "in God the Father." Paul, Silvanus, and Timothy underlined this when writing to the church at Thessalonica. They wrote that the believers were: "In God the Father and the Lord Jesus Christ." (1 Thessalonians 1:1b). The apostle Paul besought us to walk worthily of the calling wherewith we were called. Few of us believers have any idea of the magnificence, the height, the breadth, and the depth of our calling. Maybe if we had a full understanding of it, it would impact and influence the course of our lives. The Lord Jesus in His High Priestly Prayer said:

That they may all be one; even as thou, Father, art in me, and I in thee, that they also may be in us: that the world may believe that thou didst send me (John 17:21).

The Lord Jesus described this "Unity of the Spirit" as being of the same dimension and quality as the unity between God the Father and God the Son. It is staggering and beyond normal comprehension that we should have been called into the same unity as exists between the Father and the Son. This also gives us a new understanding of the desire of God to dwell among us, to find a home in us.

The Tragedy of so much in Church History

When we begin to realise the extent of this truth, we also begin to understand the tragedy of so much in church history. The fact that the church is still on this earth alive and empowered is wholly due to the builder of the church, the Lord Jesus. The tragedy is the denominational divisions which have rent the body of Christ. It is also the institutionalism and organisationalism which has made "the church" something other than God intended it to be. In fact, the "Laodicean Church" is a condition in which we find everything religiously "Christian" except the Head of the church, the Lord Jesus: He is outside of it!

They read and study His Word, they have all the rites, they label it with His Name and, unbelievably, He is excluded from the whole set up. It can exist and run without Him!

We Did Not Want to Touch Anything That Divides True Believers

When the fellowship at Halford House began to see this truth of the oneness of Christ, it overwhelmed us. We did not want to be "in" anything that divided true believers from true believers. We did not even want to touch anything that divided. We saw the Lord's Table, the breaking of bread (Communion), as a supreme witness to the oneness of Christ. From the beginning we felt that we should welcome all believers to the Table—all whom the Lord had received, whatever their label. We did not feel that it was right to investigate and interrogate believers before they were allowed to partake. For example, we did not ask believers if they had been baptised as a believer or as an infant, or whether they had spoken in a tongue, or whether they believed in a pre-tribulation rapture, or post-tribulation, or what their views were on the Millennium, etc. Our understanding was that we should love the believers and care for them, thus allowing them to find the truth themselves as the Holy Spirit taught them. It was thrilling to see the large number who grew in the Lord and came to the same understanding as we held.

By interrogating and investigating we normally halt the growth of a young or weak believer. Whereas, when such believers were loved and cared for, they themselves grew in the grace and in the knowledge of the Lord Jesus. In this way we maintained the Unity of the Spirit.

All of us refused to have any link with denominationalism. Nevertheless, those who came amongst us who belonged to different denominations we welcomed and loved.

The Church is Christ!

After I was saved through reading the biography of C.T. Studd, written by his son-in-law Norman Grubb, I was baptised in a Baptist church and became a rabid Baptist! My fellow servicemen in the Royal Air Force (R.A.F), in Egypt, had to put up with my intense zeal to make them all Baptists! It was some years later that I read a little booklet entitled, "God's Spiritual House" by T. Austin Sparks. I found it incredibly helpful. However, I came to a certain point in the book where Brother Sparks declared: "As we can see Christ is the Church" I was horrified. I had heard that he held heretical views, but in his books, some of which I had read, I had never found anything heretical. It was also the same when I had heard him speak. I closed the book and said to myself: "Now I know why people think he is a heretic. Every Christian knows that Christ is the Head of the church and the church is His body. It is entirely wrong to say that the body is also Christ."

The Humor of God

The Lord has great humour! The next morning my reading was from I Corinthians 12:12—31. It began:

For as the body is one, and hath many members,
and all the members of the body, being many,
are one body; so also is Christ (v. 12).

I was stunned; there had to be something wrong in the translation! It clearly stated that all the members of the body, however many, were Christ. I looked up a whole number of versions and found that my own version of the Bible was exactly the same as the other versions. I then checked the Greek, only to find that the various versions were correct. Suddenly the Lord said to me in my Spirit: "Your head is Lance Lambert; who is your body?" In a flash I saw the truth. In that moment I went down a Baptist and came up a Christian and have been only a Christian ever since!

Named Only "Christians"

Generally speaking, this was the view of the fellowship at Halford House. We were Christians and happy to be named so. Some years later when we were applying for the licence for the church which met at Halford House to conduct and to register marriages, the chief registrar wanted to know what denomination we were. I replied that we were Christians. He said that he could not write down the word, "Christians" because it was not a denomination! However, I argued for a while with him and finally he agreed that we should be named only "Christians." Thus, every marriage certificate at Halford House had the words, "Married according to the rites of the Christians."

We did not despise people who called themselves by denominational names, but we felt we could not sin by calling ourselves any other name than Christian.

For us this issue was not "splitting hairs," as if it really did not matter what we called ourselves. Our understanding was that it was vital and essential that we only name ourselves with the Name of Christ. To be on a clear foundation of Christ alone is vital to the building of the House of the Lord. It was also essential to the flow of Christ's life and power through His body, the church. To be involved with the historic divisions of the church, and in many cases its apostasy, would have been spiritual suicide.

It is also crucial to holding the Testimony of Jesus. From the book of Revelation we understand that it is all important that the church should hold the Testimony of Jesus during the whole course of history. It opens with the risen Messiah, the Head of the church, speaking to the seven churches. They cover the whole of church history. Each one of them was represented by the seven-branched golden lampstand, the menorah of the Tabernacle and Temple. The light borne by those lampstands is the Testimony of Jesus. When the lampstand is removed so is the Testimony of Jesus. The Presence or the withdrawal of the Testimony of Jesus is the Divine verdict on the history of the church. It signifies either the fulfilment of God's purpose or His total dissatisfaction.

Maintaining the Unity of the Spirit

It is amazing to see how divided and factionalised believers can become. It is almost as if the powers of darkness have a "Trojan horse" within the church. Throughout its history the Enemy has wrought havoc through division and faction, whether it is through large and important matters or petty issues. Jealousies, rivalries, self-seeking, backbiting and gossip have led in the end to serious division, spiritual death, and paralysis. It is incredible how small and petty are some of the roots of division. It reminds me of one of the issues that divided all the synagogues in Russia in the Middle Ages. The issue of the heated debate and the resulting division was over how many angels could stand on a pin head!

It is incredible sometimes to recognise how petty and small the issues which divide people can be. So heated do some believers become that they will not acknowledge or even speak to another believer; often for a lifetime! This is the more remarkable when we remember that the Lord Jesus, after He had given us the pattern prayer, said:

> For if ye forgive men their trespasses, your heavenly Father will also forgive you. But if ye forgive not men their trespasses, **neither will your Father forgive your trespasses** (Matthew 6:14—15 author's emphasis).

Simply stated, it means that the prayers of such believers are not heard! Such bitter divisions bring only paralysis and lifelessness to any church.

The Root of so much Division and Faction

It is no wonder that the Lord spoke about losing our self-life when He said:

If any man would come after me, let him deny himself, and
take up his cross, and follow me. For whosoever would save
his life shall lose it; and whosoever shall lose his life for my
sake and the gospel's shall save it (Mark 8:34b—35).

It is our unbroken self-life which produces pride, rivalries, jealousies, self-seeking, self protection and much else. It is only when we are prepared to lose our self-life that we shall find it under new management—His lordship. There is absolutely no way that we can maintain or keep the Unity of the Spirit where there is an unbroken self-life. It is the death knell to that Unity. The ground which Satan always uses is the flesh in any believer, whoever he or she is, great or small. It is merely a question of time before the issues appear which destroy the Unity of the Spirit and our ability to maintain it.

The Qualities Needed to Maintain the Unity of the Spirit

We should note how the Holy Spirit introduces this matter of maintaining the Unity:

With all lowliness and meekness, with longsuffering,
forbearing one another in love; giving diligence to keep the
unity of the Spirit in the bond of peace (Ephesians 4:2—3).

Such qualities enable us to overcome any situation however devilish it may be. Note carefully the qualities needed to maintain the unity of the Spirit—lowliness, meekness, longsuffering, forbearance and diligence. These are all the character of the Lord indwelling us! We should always remember that it takes **two people** to maintain division. When, on one side, the "self-life" is "lost" or "laid down," the Lord uses the presence of division and faction to sift the other side, to refine them and change them into His likeness. The apostle Paul writes:

> *For there must be also factions among you, that*
> *they that are approved may be made manifest*
> *among you (1 Corinthians 11:19)*

The problems we often face in division are the very means of nailing us to His cross and forcing us to live in His power and resurrection life.

I remember the old Puritan divine who said: "You take care of your good conscience; God will take care of your good name." These problems in the life of the church are either the means of destruction or the means of transformation. To deliberately maintain the Unity of the Spirit in the face of what could divide us brings to such a person or people spiritual growth and maturity. It is true overcoming! It is maintaining the Unity of the Spirit in action!

12.
The Lord's Great Commission

A Commission to Be Obeyed

Another truth which deeply influenced the whole fellowship at Halford House from its beginning was the subject of reaching the unsaved. Before the Lord Jesus ascended to the right hand of the Father, He gave to us all, through His apostles, the Commission, which has solemn and far reaching meaning. Jesus said:

> *All authority hath been given unto me in heaven and on earth. Go ye therefore, and make disciples of all the nations, baptizing them into the name of the Father and of the Son and of the Holy Spirit: teaching them to observe all things whatsoever I commanded you: and lo, I am with you always, even unto the end of the world (Matthew 28:18—20).*

Since His proclamation of this Commission, He has never countermanded it, changed it, or shelved it. The fellowship at Halford House, therefore, believed that the Commission remained to be obeyed; *...unto the end of the world.* We have no right to ignore it and certainly no right to disobey it. We should note that the risen Christ specifically said that this Commission is operative and effective until His return. We believed that it was our practical obedience to this command which had to lie at the heart of the work of the Lord.

Go and Make Disciples

In the charge the Lord Jesus gave us, He commanded us to: *Go...and make disciples of all the nations.* The record of Mark adds to our understanding, for he records the Lord's words: "Go ye into all the world, and preach the gospel to the whole creation." (Mark 16:15). Here there are two very important matters underlined. Firstly, we have to **go** into all the world and make disciples of all nations. We cannot ignore the fact that this is a physical "going" and not a remaining in our home. There is no excuse whatsoever for disobedience to our Lord's command. We have to thank the Lord for those who have at great cost left all and gone to the far corners of the earth to preach the gospel. The history of the church is full of such examples. The Lord's charge is still operative and extends to His return. Even if it is not His will for us "to go" but to remain, we cannot have an inward looking view rather than a world view.

Moreover this "going" is an attitude of heart and mind. We may not go to the ends of the earth but we can go across the street to our neighbours or into situations in the area in which we live. In other words, we should have a deep and living concern for the lost that they may be saved. If we remain rather than go, without any compassion at all for the unsaved world around us, we are disobeying the Lord's command. Furthermore when we have a right attitude of heart, the world will often come to us and find the salvation of the Lord through us.

Secondly, it is not "converts" we are to make but "disciples." There is a vast difference between a convert and a disciple. A disciple is someone who is wholly committed to the Lord, experiencing His salvation and resurrection life, and being taught and trained by the Lord. He or she is seeking to observe everything He commanded, which denotes a very high standard of committal and devotion to Him. If we add to this that a believer baptised into the name of the Father, and of the Son, and of the Holy Spirit, has begun to understand and experience the significance and meaning of his or her baptism, we have a disciple. A true understanding of the spiritual significance of baptism is a key to spiritual growth and maturity, and to genuine discipleship.

The Church-A Rescue Shop Within a Yard of Hell

If the command of the Lord is truly obeyed, you will have a church where the unsaved are being reached and brought to Christ, and then built up as a Spiritual House. There will always be people being saved with all the problems that often brings. It is, however, like a normal home where the family is being increased by new birth. Those babes in Christ are being nurtured, educated, and trained for adulthood. Such new life has an incredibly renewing and reviving effect on the whole household of God. In this kind of living, functioning, and growing church there is no place for "a holy huddle." Neither is there any place for producing an "elite" company of overcomers; a company of believers in which any one below par is made unwelcome. The church has its problem children, as well as those who are growing up into the full stature of Christ. Indeed, part of the growing up into that stature is the care of the problematic and difficult children in the family of God! It would be wonderful to form a company of absolutely perfect saints in which there is no problem. That, however, is not the family which the Lord is producing!

We should remember a couplet which C.T. Studd composed and which caused many Christians to be very angry with him:

"Some want to live within the sound
Of church or chapel bell.
I want to run a rescue shop
Within a yard of hell."

The fact is that the normal and healthy church which the Lord is building is so often "a rescue shop within a yard of hell." Out of that the Lord builds His House. Those who are rescued will often bring with them many problems and difficulties. Therefore, a true church can never be absolutely perfect. It will always have those who are immature or sometimes stunted in growth. This kind of situation will require much grace on the part of those who are spiritually mature.

Only the Lord can give to a company of believers a worldwide view. By nature and left to ourselves, our view becomes insular and narrowed to our own understanding and concerns. One often visits Christian groups which only circle around their own particular doctrine and teaching. One wonders whether they have ever heard the Commission of the Lord, for they are entirely caught up with their own growth and holiness. The world may be dying on their doorstep, but they have no conception or thought of it. One wonders how the Lord could ever be at home in such a group!

The Whole Counsel of God

The apostle Paul said when giving his farewell address to the church at Ephesus:

> *For I shrank not from declaring unto you the*
> *whole counsel of God (Acts 20:27).*

The problem of so many churches is that what is preached is far less than the whole counsel of God. Sometimes it is only one aspect of the whole which is given. Other times it includes more than one aspect but still not the whole. Paul spoke of the whole counsel of God. That must include the Eternal Purpose of God—the church as the Bride of Christ and as the Home of God, the need to be crucified with Christ to experience His resurrection life; intercession as fellowship with Him in the fulfilling of His will; the growth to maturity of believers; evangelistic outreach; the salvation of Israel, and many other aspects. Can we be part of the House of the Lord, which He is building, and only preach one aspect of the whole counsel of God?

When a fellowship of believers has a worldwide view, the Spirit of the Lord will begin to give them burdens for other parts of the world. In praying for the building of the House of the Lord in other regions, they will begin to discover that they are part of a worldwide fellowship of saints. In turn they will themselves be built up by the Lord.

"Fishing"

From the very beginning of the fellowship at Halford House, there was a deep concern for the unsaved world around us. When the Lord gave us a house on the lower part of Richmond Hill, we were within minutes of all the main areas of the town. Richmond is a major attraction for tourists; it has the River Thames, Richmond Hill, Richmond Park (One of London's Great Royal parks), which are a magnet for tourists and for young people. It was a perfect area for evangelism. The position of Halford House made it an ideal base from which to reach the unsaved.

On every Sunday evening about an hour before the service began, a group of our young people would have a prayer time and then go out into the streets onto the towpath of the river to reach people. We called this "fishing." It was based on the words of our Lord Jesus to Peter and Andrew: "Come ye after me, and I will make you fishers of men." (Matthew 4:19b). Over the years the Lord blessed this endeavour. Quite a number of those who became an integral part of the fellowship were "fished in" as unsaved people; even one who became my brother-in-law. We had a simple evangelistic service with some hymns which were always followed with a message. Sometimes we had testimonies or someone would sing a gospel song. Afterwards, we always served tea and biscuits followed by an aftertime of fellowship. A number of those who came were saved during those times.

The Billy Graham Crusades

It was because of our heart towards the unsaved that we fully supported the Billy Graham crusades. We hired a number of buses and advertised that, free of charge, we would take anyone to the meetings. A number of people whom we took found the Lord during those times. It was not only through the Billy Graham crusades, but also through house to house visiting that we sought to reach people for the Lord.

Some Remarkable Characters who came to the Lord

Mrs. Quinnell

I can only give a few examples from many of those who found the Lord. One of those characters who was saved amongst us was Mrs. Quinnell. In fact, she had come up on a bus we had provided to a Billy Graham crusade. She found the Lord simply and truly. She was of Irish extraction and had an enormous sense of humour. Every Sunday without fail she was amongst us, and in the evening meeting she always sat in the same place. She had a very bad cough and the stewards would give her a glass of water before the meeting. Whenever I spoke I always began by reading the portion of Scripture from which I would speak and then would say, "And now let us pray." Before I prayed I would quietly take the glass of water on the speaker's table and take a sip. On this occasion, as I took the glass, I became aware of some movement in the congregation. The place was completely packed. I had already read the Scripture, had the glass of water in my hand and was about to pray. Suddenly, I became aware that Mrs. Quinnell was standing up. Quietly, without a word, she lifted up her glass and mouthed the word, "Cheers." I was so shocked that I, without further word, lifted my glass and also mouthed the word, "Cheers." Then I prayed and preached the gospel. Mrs. Quinnell had a simple but very real faith in the Lord until she went to be with Him.

Mrs. Head

Mrs. Head was another lady who found the Lord in her retirement years. She was born in Devon and raised in Totnes. She had been the chief cook to the Duke and Duchess of Devonshire, her husband being the chief butler. In the years of her widowhood she found the Lord. It was also in a Billy Graham crusade. Her faith was simple, but absolutely real. She would always come, not only on Sundays, but also to the Bible studies.

On every Friday morning she came in to have a cup of tea with us at Halford House. On one of those occasions she suddenly announced that she was not going to read her Bible anymore with the words: "I am giving up reading my Bible." When she had come to the Lord, she had adopted a systematic reading of the Bible, beginning with Genesis and had at that point reached Revelation 12:7. When she made her announcement, I and Margaret, who was serving the tea, were shocked.

We both chorused: "Whatever is wrong?"

"Well," she said, in her rich Devonian dialect, "this morning my reading began with: *And there was war in heaven*. I have lived through two world wars and I cannot face a war in heaven!"

So I explained to her that it was not war in the future but a war that was already present.

Then she smiled and said, "I am so glad," and took up her Bible reading again.

Mrs. Head and Florrie

Mrs. Head and Florrie shared the same apartment. Florrie was the daughter of a very well known jockey and was also a Devonian. There was nothing that the two of them did not know about horses. Both of them came to the Lord amongst us.

It was on one of the Friday mornings that Mrs. Head came in for tea. Margaret was preparing the tea and I was tearing up football coupons still in their unopened envelopes, which had been sent to me and had nothing to do with me. As I tore them up Mrs. Head said, "Are those football coupons?"

"Yes," I said, "they are!"

"Florrie and I consider them a waste of time. We do not do them anymore," she said.

"Very good," I said. "Actually, one of the brothers has tried to stop them sending them to me by writing across one of the envelopes, 'Deceased,' and sending it back. However, they still send them to me!"

I had my back to Mrs. Head as I was tearing up these coupons and putting them in a waste paper basket. Then I heard her say, "But we still do the horses."

I could not believe my ears! As I turned around, shocked, Margaret was coming in with the tea.

"Mrs. Head," I said, with the most puritanical voice I could muster, "if you bring this into the Presence of the Lord you are bound to feel a disquiet."

With her china blue eyes fixed on me she said, "Florrie and I do."

"That is impossible," I said.

"Ah," she said, "but that is what we do. We studies the form in the newspaper, then we gets on our knees, and we asks our dear Lord to lead us to the right horse."

"That is impossible," I said.

"No it isn't," she said, "our dear Lord always leads us to the right horse. Every week we win."

I felt weak around the knees and Margaret nearly dropped the tea tray. "How do you think Florrie and I live on our pension?" Mrs. Head said, "it would be impossible, but for our winnings."

Both Margaret and I were speechless! Mrs. Head then continued, "When Florrie and I have our daily pint of guinness at the Marlborough Arms, the regulars come up and ask us for a tip off for the horse of the week. We give them the horse that we are backing only if they promise to give us 2% of their earnings!" Apparently, the two of them were doing quite well!

Florrie and the Missing False Teeth

On one occasion I suddenly had a phone call from Dr. Pavlevic. He treated both Mrs. Head and Florrie and always called me, "Rabbi." He was Jewish and a survivor of the Holocaust. He was in a terrible state. "Come quickly," he said, in very good English but with a Polish accent. "Florrie has had a serious heart attack, and it is very bad. The ambulance is here with the district nurse, but Florrie is refusing to go."

I asked, "Why does she refuse to go?"

Dr. Pavlevic said, "She cannot find her teeth! Mrs. Head has searched everywhere for them and cannot find them. Rabbi, you must come immediately or she vill die."

I said, "I will be there in 15 minutes." With that I told Margaret and we both went as fast as we could. It was mercifully in a street parallel with Halford Road. When we got to Mrs. Head's house we saw the ambulance with its doors open and rushed upstairs. Florrie had her hand over her mouth and never at any time took it away. Dr. Pavlevic was saying, "Stupid voman, she vill die if she does not go to the hospital soon!"

Mrs. Head said, "I have searched everywhere and I cannot find her teeth."

Then Margaret said, "Florrie, can you hear me? You must go to the hospital, because you are holding the ambulance up which might be needed for other serious cases. I will take up all the carpets, I will even take up all the floorboards if necessary, but I will find your teeth and bring them to you in the hospital."

With that Florrie agreed and was taken on the stretcher down the stairs to the ambulance with her hand still over her mouth. Dr. Pavlevic was saying repeatedly in Hebrew: "Baruch Hashem, Baruch Hashem." (Blessed be the Lord).

After Florrie had gone, Margaret and Mrs. Head searched everywhere but could not find the false teeth. Then Margaret phoned me and said, "I had better go to the hospital without her teeth and speak with her." When Margaret got to the hospital, there was Florrie with many pillows behind her because of her heart condition and a great smile on her face with her teeth intact. "Oh," Margaret said, "Florrie you have your teeth."

"Sorry," said Florrie. "I thought I had lost them when I was sick, but they must have been there all the time." By keeping her hand over her mouth she had unwittingly concealed the fact that the teeth were there all along!

I went in to see Florrie the following day. She was asleep, but I sat down beside her and prayed. The paper was open at the horses and her Bible was also open on top of the paper. That evening she passed into the Presence of the Lord. She had picked a winner on the day she died. I was so shaken by our experience with Florrie and Mrs. Head that all I could say to the fellowship at Florrie's funeral was, "I am sure Florrie said to one of the angels, 'Did my horse win?'"

At the fellowship which met at Halford House we rightly did not agree with gambling of any kind and in telling this story I am not advocating it. Nevertheless, Mrs. Head and Florrie had a simple but real faith in the Lord. They were two of the weaker members of the body, yet still precious and real. They needed to be loved and cared for in the same way that the more advanced saints were loved and cared for.

Brian and Ivy Hare

Before Ivy married Brian Hare, we had first met her in a restaurant in Richmond. She was a waitress waiting on our table. Somehow we got into conversation with her and she asked who we were. We explained that we were Christians from a fellowship in the town. She expressed real interest and said how she would love to come to one of the meetings. However, she said that she could only come on a Sunday morning because of her duties in the restaurant. So we encouraged her to come. We always had the Lord's Table on Sunday morning, and we wondered whether that was the best time for her to attend. Since it was the only time she could come to us we encouraged her to come even though she was not a believer.

We always gave a warning at the Lord's Table not to take the bread or wine unless one was a believer. During the course of that morning meeting, whilst the bread was being broken and the wine was being poured out, she saw the Lord. Instead of the brother who was breaking the bread and pouring out the wine, it was the Lord she saw, and she was wonderfully saved. From the moment she was born again, she grew in grace and in the knowledge of the Lord Jesus, and never looked back.

Not very long after finding the Lord, Ivy asked if she could see me. She said, "I cannot help noticing that none of the girls wear any make-up. But I am so pale; if I did not wear some make-up I would look as if I was dying. I will never give up my make-up for any reason!"

I said, "Ivy, you look wonderful. Who has spoken to you about make-up?"

"No one has," she said.

"Well," I said, "you can be a child of God and wear make-up or a child of God and not wear make-up. The question is whether the Lord speaks to you about it and whether you are obedient to Him." Then I said to her, "Ivy, will you promise me something?"

"Yes," she said. "Promise me you will never give up your make-up unless the Lord speaks to you."

"I certainly will," she said.

A little while later when she had obviously grown in the Lord, I noticed she wore no make-up. I spoke to her about it: "You are not wearing make-up anymore; what about the promise you made to me?"

"Oh," she said, "the Lord spoke to me about it and I gave it up." The Lord shone through her. Later Ivy became an integral part of the church.

At that time her fiancé Brian was not saved, and so we all prayed for him. Having given up her make-up and other worldly things, Ivy became very afraid that she would lose him. Then the Lord spoke to her as to whether He, the Lord, was first in her life. She had a struggle but sacrificed Brian to the Lord. Wonderfully, within a very short time, Brian found the Lord at Halford House. He asked to see me and said he was amazed at what had happened to Ivy. It had made a deep impression upon him and I was able to point him to the Lord Jesus.

In chapter three we have already written about their wedding and preparing the library for their reception. Together they made a rich and full contribution to the life of the fellowship. For a while they lived in the residential side of Halford House with the two sons God gave them, Jonathan and Nigel. They made a powerful and living contribution to the life of the fellowship.

Ivan and Blanche Hayward-Smith

Ivan and Blanche had not been long married when they attended a Billy Graham crusade meeting. As Billy Graham gave the invitation to receive the Lord as Saviour, they both went forward. Unfortunately, they were not well counselled. They had expressed their desire to follow the Lord, but no one helped them in their first steps. They had previously been going to Bible studies at a very well known Anglican church, but did not find the Lord. They were both seeking the Lord but did not find Him.

In some way Edna Clay, one of the sisters in the fellowship at Halford House, had business connections with Ivan and mentioned to him about the weekend meetings. They both came with Edna and were gloriously saved. It began with Blanche. Once again it was the issue of her make-up. The Lord spoke to Blanche about it and she gave it up. It was to be the beginning of a complete transformation of her life. Ivan watched all of this with great interest. Finally, he came to me and said that he recognised something had happened to his wife. She was a changed woman. It was a joy to point him to the Saviour. These two came to us, were saved, and never left us.

At real cost to themselves they took on the residential side of Halford House. Their ministry of hospitality was a gift of God to the whole fellowship. With Brian and Ivy they became a vital and integral part of the fellowship and its testimony.

Alan and Doreen Knight

Doreen Knight had been attending some of the meetings at Halford House and came to me one day to ask if she could borrow Watchman Nee's book, "The Normal Christian Life." Since she was not saved I was a little reluctant to give her the book. I thought that it would be better if she was saved and already growing up in the Lord. However, she was insistent and I gave her the book. Amazingly, it was through this book that Doreen gloriously found the Lord. From the moment she was saved, through the understanding the Lord gave her both of the Gospel and the Christian Life through Watchman Nee's book, she steadily grew.

Her husband Alan was baffled by the enormous change that had taken place in his wife. Pondering over the change which had taken place, the Lord met him and saved him. These two and their son Max were a real contribution to the work of the Lord at Halford House. Alan looked after the finances of the fellowship and Doreen became a real intercessor.

Making Disciples of the Lord Jesus

I have only mentioned a few of those who were saved amongst us. They illustrate the fulfilment of the Commission which the Lord gave us to preach the Gospel and to make disciples. They were not only born of God, they became disciples of the Lord Jesus. There were also many who already belonged to the Lord when they joined us and grew greatly in Him amongst us. We learnt as a fellowship that it is much easier to make a convert than a disciple. First and foremost, the only one who can make disciples is the Lord Jesus Himself. It is therefore incredible that He has commanded us to "Go," and not only preach the gospel but "to make disciples." The only way we can make disciples is in and through the Lord Jesus. That simply means there has to be deep heart transactions between the servant of the Lord and his or her Master. If there is no gold, silver or costly stones of the nature and life of the Lord Jesus in His servant, how can that servant build on the foundation of Christ gold, silver and costly stones (see 1 Corinthians 3:11–15)? What is the source of this gold, silver and costly stones? We know only too well the origin of the wood, hay and stubble! It is our flesh! To be able to minister gold, silver and costly stone requires His indwelling of us.

The Holy Spirit can only use us as His servants "to make disciples," if we are already ourselves His disciple. It means that you have become a living sacrifice. That is a costly way but leads to great and eternal reward. The cost is our self-life; only thus can the Lord bring into us the gold, silver, and the costly stones of His own life and nature.

Epilogue:
I Have Set Watchmen
upon Thy Walls,
O Jerusalem

As far as God's purpose and work is concerned, the aim of Satan never changes; always it is to kill, to steal and to destroy. Relentlessly, he works to sidetrack everything that began with the Lord. When his endeavours are successful, as so often they are, the building of the church is not only halted, but the church is turned into something which God never intended it to be. The strategy of the powers of darkness has not changed since Satan first deceived Adam and Eve. He said:

> **Indeed,** has God said, 'You shall not eat from any tree of the garden'? Satan then flatly contradicted God's Word to them and said: You **surely** shall not die! (Genesis 3:1b, 4b NASB author's emphasis).

From this successful tactic of Satan, the fall of man began. We ought to pay attention to the fact that Satan always begins by challenging God's Word, and what the Lord has revealed through it.

Satan's Strategy Over the Church

The strategy of Satan and his hierarchy concerning Christ's building of the church is incredibly the same. He has subverted every initiative which Christ has launched in the history of the church. Whilst we have no business to laud the Enemy for his success, the fact is stark! He has turned what was spiritual and heavenly in nature into something earthly, worldly, and lifeless. The Word of God declares that the Devil has the power of death (see Hebrews 2:14). With the pilgrim church his power of death has no affect whatsoever, **unless** he can first deceive and subvert her. It is this tactic of his that has been so successful. Furthermore, Satan has found a willing ally in the flesh of believers. Indeed, by that flesh he has created a "Trojan horse" within the church, through which he has won many successes.

The Initiatives of Christ in the Church's History

As I have written, every one of the initiatives which Christ has launched in the pilgrim church's long history, have been subverted by Satan within a few generations. The church which is meant to represent the Lord Jesus on earth, holding His Testimony, being the outshining of His light in the darkness, has often become the most bloody and ferocious persecutor and murderer of the pilgrim church. It is a fact of history that the prostituted church has caused the martyrdom of multitudes of faithful and precious believers of the true Church.

Nevertheless, in all these initiatives fundamental truth has been recovered never to be lost again. The enthroned Head and Builder of the True Church has ensured that! However, we have to ask ourselves the question: How has the Enemy been so successful in his strategies, especially when the triumphant Messiah is enthroned at the Father's right hand? With the total Sovereign power which the Messiah has in heaven and on this fallen earth, He could easily have thwarted Satan. Why has He not done so?

The answer to this question is simple and clear. Altogether apart from the flesh life of believers becoming a "Trojan horse" within these initiatives and thus subverting them, the triumphant Christ is supremely seeking to train His own in fellowship with Himself. He is seeking to empower us to gain the victory in the building of His Church, to take action in union with Himself. In this connection we should understand the words of **the** Builder, Christ, when He said to Peter as representing the members of His body:

> *I will give you the keys of the kingdom of heaven; and*
> *whatever you bind on earth shall have been bound in*
> *heaven, and whatever you loose on earth shall have*
> *been loosed in heaven (Matthew 16:19 NASB mg).*

We also discover this from the apostle Paul's letter to the church at Ephesus, when he wrote:

> *With all prayer and supplication praying at all seasons in*
> *the Spirit, and **watching thereunto in all perseverance** and*
> *supplication for all the saints (Ephesians 6:18 author's emphasis).*

Those words, *watching thereunto in all perseverance*, contain the key to the Enemy's success or failure in subverting these initiatives of Christ! We should mark that it is persistent watching that is required. If there is no "watching" on the part of the believers, in the end the Enemy wins! When we learn to watch with Him, through His power and grace we overcome and the work of building the Church progresses!

Wherefore Watch Ye

The prophetic words of the apostle on the last occasion he spoke to the Ephesian church gives us a further clue:

> **Take heed** unto yourselves, and to all the flock, in which the Holy Spirit hath made you overseers, to feed the church of the Lord which he purchased with his own blood. I know that after my departing grievous wolves shall enter in among you, not sparing the flock; and from among your own selves shall men arise, speaking perverse things, to draw away the disciples after them. **Wherefore watch ye** (Acts 20:28—31a mg author's emphasis).

This prophecy of Paul was totally fulfilled in the ensuing history of the church at Ephesus. Amongst Bible scholars it is generally recognised that the Ephesian letter is the high tide water mark of biblical revelation in the New Testament concerning God's Eternal Purpose and the Church. If such a church as Ephesus could fall completely, so can any other! Certainly this has happened with every initiative which the Lord has since taken until the present day. We therefore should take serious note of these warnings.

Warning from the Head of the Church

Furthermore, it is the glorified and risen Lord Jesus, the Head of the church, who also Himself warned the church at Ephesus that He would come and move their lampstand out of its place unless they repented. He had first strongly commended them, but then went on to say:

> But I have this against thee, that **thou didst leave thy
> first love.** Remember therefore whence **thou art fallen,
> and repent** and do the first works; or else I come to thee,
> and will move thy lampstand out of its place, **except thou
> repent** (Revelation 2:4—5 mg author's emphasis).

For the Lord to have used the words, thou art fallen, and repent, repeating them again, except thou repent, gives us an understanding that the church at Ephesus was at a turning point. His use of the word repent should have been enough to warn the church of serious problems within it. It was in fact a solemn word of counsel for those with ears to hear what the Spirit was saying to that church.

The Sad Fact That Ephesus Did Not Take Heed

Is it any wonder that the Lord Jesus, through the apostle Paul, prophetically told them to take heed unto yourselves, and wherefore watch ye. We have the same sense of warning when Paul wrote in his letter to the church in Ephesus:

> Finally, be strong in the Lord, and in the strength of his
> might. Put on the whole armor of God, that ye may be able to
> stand against the wiles of the devil (Ephesians 6:10—11).

Did the church take heed? Did they take serious note of this continual emphasis on watching? Did they put on the whole armour of God so that they would not be deceived or subverted by the wiles or stratagems of the Devil? Did they hear that solemn and biting Word from the risen Messiah? *Thou didst leave thy first love. Remember therefore whence thou art fallen, and repent.* Sadly they did not! If they had been alert and awake, maybe the stratagem of the Devil would have failed. As it was they did not hear with a hearing ear and the lampstand was removed. It is not only the church at Ephesus who lost the Testimony of Jesus, but every movement of the Holy Spirit which the Lord has initiated in the building, recovery and restoration of His church. It was the quenching of the work of the Spirit and the enthronement of flesh among them which brought those moves of the Spirit to an end.

The Burglary at the Halford House

This solemn and disturbing truth came home to us in the fellowship at Halford House through a small and seemingly nonsensical burglary! It was the only burglary which we experienced, but it had a profound impact upon us all. One night a slim burglar managed to squeeze himself through a very small toilet window which had been carelessly left unlatched. From the entrance hallway he stole a whole mantelshelf of brass and copper, including a Georgian hand beaten copper plate which was valuable. He went out in the same way he came in, taking the stolen goods with him. He was never found and the items were not recovered despite our reporting the burglary to the police.

This incident, as I have said, had a great impact on us all. We sought the Lord for an understanding of what He was saying to us through it. What came home to us was the fact that we needed to be alive and alert, to guard the revelation of Himself, the spiritual wealth which the Lord had given to us, and to be watchful over it.

There is so much in the Word of God about the necessity of watching. If we do not watch we most certainly will lose most, if not all of the spiritual riches He has given us, ending up as spiritual paupers. We will join the wreckage and debris of so much in church history. We have already pointed out the solemn charge of the Lord, **to watch.** If we are not alive and alert as watchmen we can lose our first love without realising it. That quality of love will have slipped away into casualness and carelessness, a kind of familiarity with the Lord and with spiritual matters. We will then be totally unaware of the danger that the lampstand will be moved out of its place.

So often it is the smallest deviation from a spiritual principle which leads in the end to backsliding and, finally, even to apostasy. For this reason the Word of God underlines the necessity of being awake and of watching!

Abide Ye Here and Watch with Me

The disciples learnt this in a very painful and dramatic manner. The Lord Jesus was approaching the greatest crisis of His human life. He desperately needed the fellowship of those disciples. When He had come into the garden of Gethsemane, He had said to them: "My soul is exceeding sorrowful, even unto death: abide ye here, and watch with me (Matthew 26:38b)." Then He took Peter, James and John with Him, leaving the others somewhere else in the garden. Whilst in agony He prayed, but they all fell asleep. His words had no impact upon them. Not one of them seemed aware of the crisis **He** was facing or the danger **they** were in. For the disciples were also to face the greatest crisis in their lives up to that point. When they were put to the test, they all panicked, fled and denied Him. The Lord Jesus had specifically told them: "Abide ye here, and watch with me."

They did not heed His word! They all fell asleep. When the Lord found them asleep, He said: "Watch and pray, that ye enter not into temptation." (see Matthew 26:38, 41). This Greek word *Peirasmos,* translated by the English word *temptation,* means "putting to the proof" or "testing." By not heeding the Lord's word to them and falling asleep, the disciples were led, unprepared, into the greatest test of their lives.

Who Was the Watchful Young Man?

Who was it that remained awake and recorded for us the words which Jesus spoke at the height of His agony? It was not the disciples, for they had slept through it. Was it the young man wearing his tallit which was torn off him by the Temple guard as he fled? Whoever it was, he was probably the one who had the key of the owners of the garden of Gethsemane. Was it John Mark? We do not know, but we are thankful for him. We learn from him the exact words which Jesus used and the enormous pressure and stress that led Jesus to sweat great drops of blood (see Mark 14:51–52 cp. Luke 22:42–44). What we do know is that totally unaware, the apostles all slept through the greatest crisis in the human life of our Lord Jesus; unaware also of the crisis they themselves were about to face. They neither supported Him nor helped Him. He faced it alone.

The Consequences of Not Watching

When we are not watchful, neither alive, nor alert, we can miss some of the greatest events spiritually that are taking place. We move through them like zombies, neither seeing nor hearing. It is in this way that the Enemy subverts these great moves of the Holy Spirit in the history of the church. No matter where you turn in that history you find the evidence of this. What was once spiritually alive to the Lord, in union with Him, hearing Him and obeying Him, has been replaced with a human organisation which neither hears nor sees. In this manner these initiatives of the Lord are paralysed. Even worse, they are turned into something totally different from that which the Lord intended.

The Lynmouth Disaster of 1952

We have a dramatic illustration of this in the Lynmouth disaster of 1952. It was one of the worst river disasters in British history. The area of Lynton and Lynmouth on the North Devon coast is one of the most beautiful and picturesque areas of Great Britain. Exmoor, which lies above Lynton and Lynmouth, is one of the great National Parks of England managed by the National Trust. The town of Lynmouth straddles the confluence of the West Lyn and East Lyn rivers in a spot known as Watersmeet. It is in a gorge 700 feet below the town of Lynton.

On the 15th and 16th of August 1952, a storm of tropical intensity broke over south-west England. The storm deposited nine inches of rain within twenty-four hours on an already waterlogged Exmoor. It has been estimated that 90 million tons of rain fell on Exmoor in those hours. The flood waters built up to 30 feet behind bridges blocked with boulders, trees and debris, and finally swept down onto Lynmouth. 34 people died in the flood and a further 420 people were made homeless. 100 buildings were destroyed, as well as 28 of the 31 bridges in the Lyn valley, and 38 cars were washed out to sea.

The Lesson We Learn from This Disaster

The course of the River Lyn had been changed by a culvert which was constructed in order to gain land on the river bed for the building of business premises in Lynmouth. When the 30 foot high flood descended on the town of Lynmouth, the culvert was soon choked with flood debris, and the water overflowed everything. It swept away all that had been built on the reclaimed land.

Although this happened sixty years ago, the death and the destruction it caused can only sadden us. Nevertheless, it is a dramatic illustration of what has happened in the course of church history. Each initiative which the Lord Jesus undertook has been paralysed and destroyed within approximately six or seven generations, about two centuries; sometimes within one or two generations! What was living and organic in nature, a practical union between the Head and the body, was destroyed by the flesh. It was human programmes and human organisations which took the place of spiritual life and power. The organic nature of the church became institutionalised and the church lost its heavenly calling. The one body in Christ became a divided, denominationalised structure, and the church was transformed into an earthly and worldly institution.

The Lynmouth disaster is a vivid and dramatic illustration of what we have mentioned so far. When the flood of water came, it returned to the original river bed and swept everything away that had been built in its path. Even the culvert which had been constructed is a picture of seeking to restrict the resurrection life and power of Christ; choking its spontaneity by trapping it in human organisation, techniques and methodology. It is nothing but the flesh in action! The fact is that the river had returned to its original course! In each initiative of the Lord

Jesus, the overflowing flood of His resurrection life and power returns the church to its original principles, foundation and character.

Christ's Initiatives and Their Universal Characteristics

In the first and second generations of each initiative which the Lord has birthed, all the characteristics of the early church returned and were expressed.

Firstly: The absolute and Practical Headship of Christ. There was no other Head and the whole body remained in practical union with Him. He was, in fact, Head! He was heard and obeyed.

Secondly: The Proclamation that Jesus is Lord. It was the Declaration that He had Sovereign Authority both in heaven and over this fallen earth. He has the keys of death and hell! With Him nothing is impossible.

Thirdly: The Fellowship of Believers. This was expressed in the practical contribution of all the members of the body. It was the Priesthood of all Believers in action.

Fourthly: The Unity of the church. It was "One body in Christ." This Unity of the Spirit had to be practically maintained.

Fifthly: The Absolute Authority of God's Word, its inspiration and relevance. It was the sole authority; not worldly wisdom or philosophy or fashion.

Sixthly: The Empowering and Leadership of the Holy Spirit. Practically, it was understood that there could be no union with the Head nor with one another in Him, apart from the Holy Spirit.

Seventhly: A Burden for the unsaved world. There was an emphasis on the salvation of the unsaved and reaching them; the preaching of the Gospel in power, and the impact of that preaching upon national and world society.

All these characteristics appeared in the beginning of each initiative which the Lord Jesus, the Builder of the true Church, launched. It is interesting to note that there is an essential unity which binds all those who were pioneers in each move of the Holy Spirit.

The Sure and Certain Final Presentation of the Bride by the Lord Jesus

These moves of the Lord have kept alive the true pilgrim church throughout the millennia of her history. If it had not been for them, the church would have died and become something altogether different from what the Lord had intended it to be. Instead, we see a recovery of living truth time after time in all these movements of the Holy Spirit. Furthermore, the truth recovered in each of them has never again been lost! The risen glorified Messiah has fulfilled the promise He made when He said:

> *Upon this rock I will build my church; and **the gates of hell shall not prevail against it** (Matthew 16:18b author's emphasis).*

Satan and his host may seem to have been successful in their attempt to subvert each move of God. In fact, the enthroned Messiah Jesus has overcome every satanic attempt, and restored essential truth to the pilgrim church. Furthermore, the Lord Jesus will finally present to His Father, His Bride without spot or wrinkle. The fulfilment of God's Eternal Purpose is secure in the hands of the Lord Jesus.

The Watchmen of the Lord Seeks

We cannot conclude this book on the recovery and restoration of the church, without returning to the necessity of being **Watchmen**! Truth which has been recovered by the Holy Spirit has to be guarded. We have to take heed to ourselves and put on the whole armour of God that we may stand against the wiles and stratagems of the Devil. We need to learn the lessons of church history and remember the old saying: "The only thing we learn from history is that we never learn from history." There is no excuse for the Enemy's success in subverting and paralysing each move of the Spirit in the building of Christ's church. All the grace and power of a Risen and Enthroned Messiah is available to us. **His victory** is meant to be **our victory**. We should not be demoralised by Satan's seeming success, but instead be standing in and for the total victory of the Messiah Jesus. He challenges us to be overcomers with Him!

For Zion's Sake Will I Not Hold My Peace-They Shall Never Hold Their Peace

The work of the Lord at Halford House began as a result of the Hebrides Revival. It also began when independently the Holy Spirit placed the same Scripture from Isaiah 62 on the hearts of eight people. We understood then, that this Scripture was referring to the New Jerusalem which is above, the mother of us all. In other words, it is the church which the Lord Jesus is at present building (see Revelation 21:2–3, 10–11 cp. Galatians 4:26 KJV). Later we understood that it also referred to the physical Jerusalem and the recreated State of Israel. Therefore it has a double prophetic meaning and fulfilment.

The Scripture placed on our hearts was:

For Zion's sake will I not hold my peace, and for Jerusalem's sake
I will not rest, until her righteousness go forth as brightness, and
her salvation as a lamp that burneth. And the nations shall see
thy righteousness, and all kings thy glory (Isaiah 62:1—2a).

And:

I have set watchmen upon thy walls, o Jerusalem;
they shall never hold their peace day nor night: ye
that are the Lord's remembrancers, take ye no rest,
and give him no rest, till he establish, and till he make
Jerusalem a praise in the earth (verses 6—7).

It was a sobering and challenging revelation to us that these watchmen He had set on the walls of Jerusalem were to have the same burden that the Messiah has. He had said: "will I not hold my peace ... I will not rest, until (see verse 1)." Of the watchmen He said: "They shall never hold their peace day nor night ... take ye no rest, and give him no rest, till he establish, and till he make Jerusalem a praise in the earth." The intense burden on the heart of the Christ is transferred and shared with the watchmen! His heart and the burden within it are to be the burden on our heart. It is staggering that the Lord Jesus will not build up Jerusalem and make her what she should be—a light to the unsaved and a praise amongst the nations—without His watchmen. They are to share His vision and burden! Here is the challenge of the Lord to be His watchmen on the walls of Jerusalem.

It is of great interest to me that the Lord called me to Israel and to Jerusalem, where I now live. In my estimation the Purpose of God for the Church cannot be completed without "the natural branches" being re-ingrafted into their own olive tree (see Romans 11:17—26). The huge conflict and battle in the Middle East and the world over Israel and Jerusalem is related to this! Satan and the powers of darkness know only too well that they have to prevent and block the salvation of Israel. The "re-ingrafting" of the Jewish people will signal the completion of the circle of world redemption and the fulfilment of God's Purpose for the Church. Is it any wonder that there is an enormous conflict and controversy over it?! The fact that Satan has engineered so much war and conflict, and much more to come, is an evidence of how vital is the salvation of Israel to God's Eternal Purpose.

We do not know how long we have before the Rapture of the saints and the Return of the Lord, or whether there will be more moves of His Spirit. It seems clear that if His church is to be built from the Foundation to the Top Stone, we will need a further powerful move of the Spirit of God which will carry us into the public coming of the Kingdom of God. If the Church is to be what He intended it to be, if the Bride of Christ is to make herself ready, we need to hear His call and His challenge to be watchmen on the walls of Jerusalem. We need not only to hear, but to respond with total devotion and commitment to Him. Thus we shall be empowered, anointed, and filled with His Spirit, and we will see His Purpose for the Church finally completed.

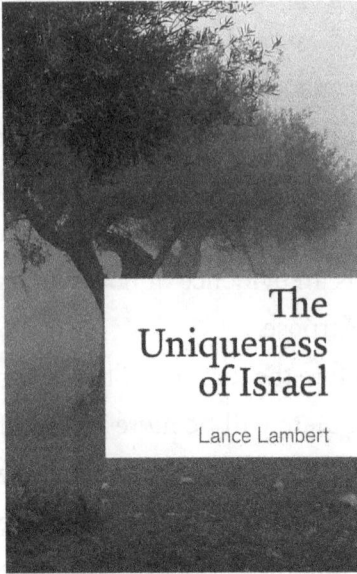

The Uniqueness of Israel

Woven into the fabric of Jewish existence there is an undeniable uniqueness. There is bitter controversy over the subject of Israel, but time itself will establish the truth about this nation's place in God's plan. For Lance Lambert, the Lord Jesus is the key that unlocks Jewish history He is the key not only to their fall, but also to their restoration. For in spite of the fact that they rejected Him, He has not rejected them.

Till The Day Dawns

Lance Lambert

Till the Day Dawns

"And we have the word of prophecy made more sure; whereunto ye do well that ye take heed, as unto a lamp shining in a dark place, until the day dawn, and the day-star arise in your hearts." (II Peter 1:9).

The word of prophecy was not given that we might merely be comforted but that we would be prepared and made ready. Let us look into the Word of God together, searching out the prophecies, that the Day-Star arise in our hearts until the Day dawns.

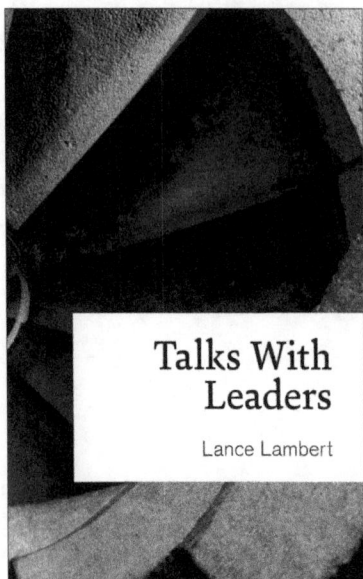

Talks With
Leaders

Lance Lambert

Talks With Leaders

"O Timothy, guard that which is committed unto thee ..."
(1 Timothy 6:20) Has God given you something? Has God
deposited something in you? Is there something of Himself
which He has given to you to contribute to the people of God?
Guard it. Guard that vision which He has given you. Guard
that understanding that He has so mercifully granted to you.
Guard that experience which He has given that it does not
evaporate or drain away or become a cause of pride. Guard that
which the Lord has given to you by the Holy Spirit. In these heart-
to-heart talks with leaders Lance Lambert covers such topics as
the character of God's servants, the way to serve, the importance
of anointing, and hearing God's voice. Let us consider together
how to remain faithful with what has been entrusted to us.

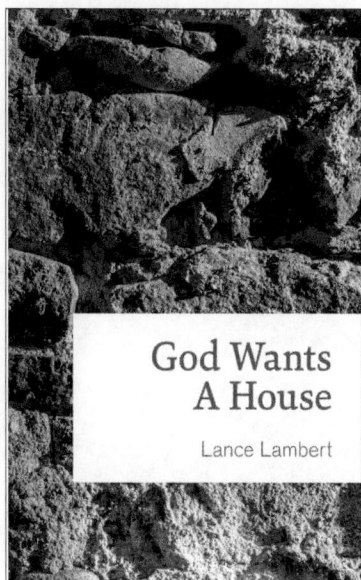

God Wants a House

Where is God at home? Is He at home in Richmond, VA?
Is He at home in Washington? Is He at home in Richmond, Surrey?
Is He at home in these other places? Where is God at home?
There are thousands of living stones, many, many dear believers
with real experience of the Lord, but where has the ark come
home? Where are the staves being lengthened that God has finally
come home? In God Wants a House Lance looks into this desire of
the Lord, this desire He has to dwell with His people. What would
this dwelling look like? Let's seek the Lord, that we can say with
David, "One thing have I asked of Jehovah, that will I seek after:
that I may dwell in the house of Jehovah all the days of my life,
To behold the beauty of Jehovah, And to inquire in his temple."

www.ingramcontent.com/pod-product-compliance
Lightning Source LLC
LaVergne TN
LVHW051254080426
835509LV00020B/2976